The Rhetorical Form

of Carlyle's

Sartor Resartus

GERRY H. BROOKES

The Rhetorical Form
of Carlyle's
Sartor Resartus

University of California Press
Berkeley, Los Angeles, London

University of California Press
Berkeley and Los Angeles, California

University of California Press, Ltd.
London, England

ISBN: 0–520–02213–0
Library of Congress Catalog Card Number: 71–185974
Printed in the United States of America

For Anne

Contents

Acknowledgments

I owe thanks to a number of people. Professor Herbert Sussman suggested this topic in the first place. Professors James L. Battersby and William J. Brandt read an earlier version of this study, my University of California dissertation, and made helpful suggestions. The staff of the Hawthorne-Longfellow Library at Bowdoin College helped me to use the collection of Carlyle materials housed there. The University of Nebraska Research Council provided a grant to aid in preparing the manuscript. Professors George E. Wolf and Charles W. Mignon listened to my arguments, offered encouragement, and read through the manuscript for me. My greatest debts are to Professor Ralph Wilson Rader, for benevolent guidance and criticism, and to Anne B. Brookes for help of all kinds.

1: The Problem of Form

> *Sartor Resartus* purports to be a book of
> philosophy, but like the fabled Proteus it
> has a way of slipping out of every cate-
> gory to which we are inclined to assign
> it.
>
> WILLIAM SAVAGE JOHNSON[1]

Sartor Resartus is a difficult work to classify. The book
seems didactic, but it contains fictions and what looks
suspiciously like narrative. Yet its fictions do not seem
to determine its structure, nor, for that matter, do its
ideas, which do not seem to be arranged according to any
simple or logical principle. The lack of simple sequence
and order in the arrangement of materials and the presence of sustained fictions in *Sartor* make it difficult to
decide whether the book is a novel or other form of narrative fiction, some form of essay or work governed
simply by ideas, or a mixed mode of questionable unity.

Usually *Sartor* has been considered one of three kinds
of works, a novel or narrative work, a work of expression, or a simple vehicle for ideas. Those who have called
it a novel have been encouraged by Carlyle's letter to
James Fraser of 27 May 1833, in which he says that
Sartor is "put together in the fashion of a kind of Didactic
Novel; but indeed properly *like* nothing yet extant."[2]

[1] "Introduction" to *Sartor Resartus: The Life and Opinions of
Herr Teufelsdröckh* (Boston: Houghton Mifflin, 1924), p. 8.

[2] The letter was first published by Charles Eliot Norton in 1888

Some critics, in a similar manner, have emphasized *Sartor's* uniqueness as a novel.[3] Other critics have applied criteria appropriate to novelistic criticism more rigorously and have disagreed about the quality and effectiveness of the work.[4]

---

in his edition of *Letters of Thomas Carlyle: 1826–1836* (London: Macmillan, 1888), II, 103–08. This work will be cited in the text as *Letters*. Charles Frederick Harrold reprints this letter in his edition of *Sartor Resartus: The Life and Opinions of Herr Teufels-dröckh* (New York: Odyssey Press, 1937), pp. 303–04. References to *Sartor* in the text are to this edition. This edition rather than the standard Centenary Edition has been cited because of the usefulness of its notes and apparatus.

[3] Thus, in the preface to his edition of *Sartor*, Archibald Mac-Mechan calls it "a novel,—with appendixes fore and aft"; *Sartor Resartus*, Atheneum Press Series (Boston: Ginn and Co., 1896), p. xli. Morse Peckham says that it is "a novel, such a novel as had never been written before" in *Beyond the Tragic Vision: The Quest for Identity in the Nineteenth Century* (New York: G. Braziller, 1962), p. 178. Charles Richard Sanders calls *Sartor* "a highly fantastic and imaginative Romantic novel in a philosophical vein" in "The Byron Closed in *Sartor Resartus*," *SIR*, 3 (1964), 81. J. W. Smeed calls it a "novel" which "represents a more or less arbitrary imposition of epic form on a part-serious, part-ironic statement of ideas" in "Thomas Carlyle and Jean Paul Richter," *CL*, 16 (1964), 230. See also Smeed's "Carlyles Jean-Paul-Ubersetzungen," *Deutsche Verteljahrsschrift für Literaturwissenschaft und Geistesgeschichte* (1961), pp. 262–79. For Carlyle's own attitude toward novels, see *Sartor*, Book Third, Chapter X; Matthew Whiting Rosa, *The Silver Fork School: Novels of Fashion Preceding "Vanity Fair"* (New York: Columbia Univ. Press, 1936); and Carlisle Moore, "Thomas Carlyle and Fiction, 1822–1834," in *Nineteenth Century Studies*, ed. Herbert Davis, William C. De-Vane, and R. C. Bald (Ithaca: Cornell Univ. Press, 1940), pp. 131–77.

[4] In "Relationship of Style and Device in *Sartor Resartus*" Daniel P. Deneau argues that *Sartor* is structured as a fictional representation of an editor editing texts and manuscripts and is flawed because the style of expression of each character is not

Those who see *Sartor* as a work of "expression" explain and perhaps justify it as a work that reveals its author's character, that exposes his ideas and his personality for all to see, that is unified by its origin in Carlyle's mind and spirit. The view is, of course, encouraged by the knowledge that in the *Reminiscences* and in remarks recorded in James Anthony Froude's biography of him, Carlyle identified incidents in *Sartor* as autobiographical.[5] Froude himself said, mistakenly, that the book was written in tumultuous haste and was as a result "defective as a work of art" but was "for that very reason a revelation of Carlyle's individuality."[6] The ten-

---

distinguished consistently from that of the others. In "The Artistic Unity of *Sartor Resartus*" John Lindberg argues that it is an unflawed novel about Teufelsdröckh, the central conflict of which is "the imperfect sympathy of the Editor for his Philosopher, and the radical inability of the Philosopher to express himself in terms acceptable to his editor." The two articles in question are published under the title "The Art of *Sartor Resartus*: Two Views," *VN*, No. 17 (spring 1960), pp. 17–23. The quotation is from p. 21. Both critics make consistency of representation a crucial element in their evaluation, as does Georg B. Tennyson implicitly. In *Sartor Called Resartus: The Genesis, Structure, and Style of Thomas Carlyle's First Major Work* (Princeton: Princeton Univ. Press, 1965), pp. 174–76, Tennyson insists that *Sartor* is "a continuous story involving human relationships in a sustained illusion of a world" and that the Editor is the protagonist of the novel. This book will be cited hereafter as *Sartor Called Resartus*.

[5] *Reminiscences by Thomas Carlyle*, ed. James Anthony Froude, 2 vols. (New York: Harper, 1881); and Froude, *Thomas Carlyle: A History of His Life in London, 1834–1881*, 2 vols. (New York: Scribner's, 1884; first edition, London: Longmans, Green, 1884).

[6] *Thomas Carlyle: A History of the First Forty Years of His Life, 1795–1835* (New York: Scribner's 1882), II, 104. Herbert J. C. Grierson says *Sartor* is "autobiography" and "if it is also more, biography, history, essays on the social questions of the day" in "Thomas Carlyle," Annual Lecture on a Master Mind, *Proc. British*

dency to see *Sartor* as expression or autobiography, however, did not begin when Carlyle's statements about its
autobiographical elements became public. Early critics
saw Book Second as "spiritual autobiography" without
knowledge of Carlyle's life. And modern critics have felt
the work is expressive independent of actual correspon-
dences between details in it and in Carlyle's life.[7] Not

Acad., 26 (1940), 305. Victor Basch says that *Sartor* is "l'auto-
biographie de la pensée de Carlyle" in *Carlyle: L'Homme et
l'oeuvre* (Paris: Gallimard, 1938), p. 124. Norwood Young calls
it "a poem of self" in *Carlyle: His Rise and Fall* (London: Duckworth, 1927), p. 114. And H. D. Traill says *Sartor* is "autobiographical from first to last. It is unquestionably a minute and
faithful history of Carlyle's intellectual and spiritual experiences,
which, of course, is the main thing" in "Introduction" to the Centenary Edition of *Sartor*, Vol. I of *The Works of Thomas Carlyle*,
ed. Traill (London: Chapman and Hall, 1896–1901), p. xviii. All
references to Carlyle's *Works* in the text are to the Centenary
Edition.

[7] Most of these critics argue additionally that *Sartor* is not a
novel. Charles Frederick Harrold feels that even in Book Second
Carlyle avoids "the problems of the novelist—effective dialogue,
organic plot, the interplay of characters" (*Sartor*, p. xxxi). He
classifies it as "philosophical poetry" (*Sartor*, p. lix) and tends to
describe it often in his "Introduction" as a work of expression.
Carlisle Moore, who appears to see *Sartor* as an expression of Carlyle's eccentricities, agrees that it lacks narrative and that "its fic-
titious elements serve other purposes than those of the novel"
("Thomas Carlyle and Fiction, 1822–1834," p. 153). George Levine
sees in *Sartor* an absence of careful narrative in "*Sartor Resartus*
and the Balance of Fiction," in *The Boundaries of Fiction: Carlyle,
Macaulay, Newman* (Princeton: Princeton Univ. Press, 1968), pp.
19–78 (an earlier version of this essay appeared in *VS*, 8 [1964],
131–60). Levine calls the book, in the terms of Northrop Frye,
"confession-anatomy-romance" (p. 23) and sees it primarily as expression, self-expression. See Frye, *Anatomy of Criticism: Four Essays* (Princeton: Princeton Univ. Press, 1957). Leonard Deen describes *Sartor* as fictional biography which incorporates autobiog-

everyone, however, has felt as Froude did that what are called *Sartor*'s expressive qualities are qualities to be admired. An early critic, Joseph Hartwell Barrett, called *Sartor*'s form expressive, but he took a rather dim view of it. Barrett felt that the work is an expression of a mind struggling out of a diseased state. He conceded that the book is what Carlyle's admirers had called it, " 'a sort of spiritual autobiography.' With this key, the interpretation is comparatively easy—the peculiarities of thought and expression, and the wild unrest everywhere manifested are with no great difficulty accounted for."[8] Considering *Sartor* a work of expression casts back any doubts about the coherence and quality of the work onto the mind that created it.

Those who have considered *Sartor* simply as a vehicle for ideas have the sanction of numbers and of intuition. Ideas, in readily quotable form, lie waiting on every page. Few would question the legitimacy of the use of the book as a source of ideas, but its use in this manner circum-

---

raphy and "anatomy" in "Irrational Form in *Sartor Resartus*," *TSLL*, 5 (1963), 441, 443. Deen also remarks that its "form is more human-expressive than perfect" (p. 449). Alvan S. Ryan sees in *Sartor* different elements, "the fictive, the expository, and the confessional," which "are not fully harmonized," and he finds the work "subjective" in "Carlyle, Jeffrey, and the 'Helotage' Chapter of *Sartor Resartus*," *VN*, No. 27 (spring 1965), p. 32. Deen's and Ryan's terms also owe something to Frye. Albert J. LaValley sees the book as an act of creation, as the expression of a quest for meaning, concurrent with the making of the book in his "*Sartor Resartus*: The Prophet Finds His Literary Role," in *Carlyle and the Idea of the Modern: Studies in Carlyle's Prophetic Literature and Its Relations to Blake, Nietzsche, Marx, and Others* (New Haven: Yale Univ. Press, 1968), pp. 69–118.

[8] "Sartor Resartus," *American Review*, 9 (N.S. 3) No. 14 (1849), 121–22.

vents certain crucial problems about the book's form and
its quality. Ideas are present, but what of their arrangement? If *Sartor* is to be isolated from other legitimate
sources of a man's ideas—his letters and his journals, for
example—and considered as literature, the coherence and
arrangement of the materials, the art of the book, must
be described. If one considers *Sartor* a vehicle for ideas,
one will meet serious difficulties in explaining or justify-
ing the relationship between the particular vehicle and
the ideas. Often the book's arrangement and its fictions
have been considered a barrier to understanding. Many
early critics felt that the fictions of *Sartor* were a mere
ornament or perhaps an obstruction to the ideas. In his
preface to the 1836 American edition of *Sartor*, Emerson
spoke of the book's "gay costume," which is nonetheless
"superficial" (*Sartor*, p. 324). Emory Neff finds that "the
detailed development" of Carlyle's view in Book Third
of *Sartor* "requires for clearness a regrouping of Carlyle's
materials that disregards the rather haphazard order of
his chapters."[9] If, as these attitudes suggest, *Sartor's*
fictions are not important and its arrangement is arbitrary, its ideas must bear great weight if the book is to
survive.[10]

[9] *Carlyle* (New York: W. W. Norton, 1932), p. 125. Cited hereafter as Neff. Louis Cazamian in *Carlyle*, tr. E. K. Brown (New
York: Macmillan, 1932), also says that in order to give an account
of the contents of the book one must adopt a simpler order than
Carlyle's (p. 104).

[10] A modern view of *Sartor* of a different sort, which is perhaps
more widely held than expressed in print, is Michael St. John
Packe's in his *The Life of John Stuart Mill* (London: Secker and
Warburg, 1954). He finds the work barely worthy of consideration:
"It was absolutely without form, devoid of coherent exposition,

Sartor has distinguishable elements and qualities, the reconciliation of which is not apparent. It has sustained fictions, something akin to narrative, important ideas, and qualities in its rhetoric that lead many to call it expressive. What we need to understand is exactly how the parts of *Sartor*—its fictions, its arrangement, its ideas—fit together in relation to the effect the whole is intended to have and to understand what that effect is.[11] The model offered here of *Sartor* as a persuasive essay may allow us to see more clearly how all of the parts of the book work together to produce one effect.[12]

---

and couched in a quite unprecedented jargon. It consisted of three parts, loosely strung together by unintelligible narrative" (p. 167).

[11] R. D. McMaster's article, "Criticism of Civilization in the Structure of *Sartor Resartus*," *UTQ*, 37 (1968), 268–80, is a partial attempt to do so. He sees the parts of the book as acting together to force the reader to see Teufelsdröckh and his times from different perspectives.

[12] A further word about G. B. Tennyson's *Sartor Called Resartus* is needed because one of his major attempts is to resolve the structural problems of *Sartor*. Tennyson has solved many other problems and brought to light new material, and critics, scholars, and readers of *Sartor* will be indebted to him, as I am. But Tennyson constructs and conflates at least four structural models for *Sartor*, making much of what he says confused and confusing. He argues that the work has organic form, that it grows out of the conditions under which it was created and out of itself or out of the premises of the beginning of the work. This model of *Sartor* allows Tennyson to explain, or at least to appear to explain, anything in the book, by reference to something prior in Carlyle's experience or by simple reference to some condition established early in the book. Tennyson also uses a musical metaphor, describing *Sartor* as a display of themes and passages that appear and reappear. Tennyson also sees *Sartor* as a work determined in part by ideas and a persuasive intention. He shows, for example, how Carlyle's style is rhetorical and supports the Clothes Philosophy. Tennyson does not, however, show how these models of *Sartor* fit to-

Sartor Resartus is a form of persuasive essay.[13] It is designed to move the reader to believe in and to act by a view of the universe that will bring him hope now and bring his society in time a new and higher form. The primary ideas that compose this view of the universe are that the world is essentially one, spiritual and divine; that we in this world know and are united by real symbols, through which we can perceive more or less dimly the divine universe; that history is passing through a regenerative period; that it is a man's duty to work earnestly without fear, at perceiving the divine world if he is able or at the task immediately before him if he can do no more; and that we must unite with other men of faith to prevent disruption of the natural course of history, to ensure the growth of an organically unified, hierarchical

gether or how *Sartor*, being all of these things, could produce a unified effect. It seems possible to be more precise, to offer a model that shows how all of the parts of *Sartor* work together to produce one effect.

[13] The critical basis of this study may be found in Ronald S. Crane, "The Concept of Plot and the Plot of *Tom Jones*," in *Critics and Criticism*, Abridged Edition (Chicago: Univ. of Chicago Press, 1957), pp. 62–93; Elder Olson, "William Empson, Contemporary Criticism, and Poetic Diction," *ibid.*, pp. 24–61; *idem, Tragedy and the Theory of Drama* (Detroit: Wayne State Univ. Press, 1966); *idem*, "Rhetoric and the Appreciation of Pope," *MP*, 37 (1939), 13–35; Wayne C. Booth, *The Rhetoric of Fiction* (Chicago: Univ. of Chicago Press, 1961), cited in the text as Booth; Ralph W. Rader and Sheldon Sacks, *Essays: An Analytic Reader* (Boston: Little, Brown, 1964); Sheldon Sacks, *Fiction and the Shape of Belief: A Study of Henry Fielding, with Glances at Swift, Johnson, and Richardson* (Berkeley: Univ. of California Press, 1964), cited in the text as Sacks; and Ralph W. Rader, "Literary Form in Factual Narrative: The Example of Boswell's *Johnson*," in *Essays in Eighteenth-Century Biography*, ed. Philip B. Daghlian (Bloomington: Indiana Univ. Press, 1968), pp. 3–42.

society out of the ashes of the present one. This set of ideas is the Clothes Philosophy. These are the premises on which Carlyle's arguments are based.

The power of *Sartor*, however, lies not simply in the intrinsic force of the Clothes Philosophy but in Carlyle's particular persuasive statement of this set of ideas. The power of his statement of the Clothes Philosophy depends on the quality and arrangement of his arguments and on his unusual use of fictions. The work is organized not as a philosophical proof or simple explanatory essay, but as a complex exhortation to belief and action. It belongs in the class of persuasive essays, but it differs from most of its kind because its argument is conducted through sustained fictions.

Sartor is not a novel because its narrative is not consistent, because its characters and other fictions do not have the intrinsic and sustained interest that fictions have in a novel but serve the persuasive purpose of the whole work. Similarly, *Sartor* is not an apologue, a work like *Rasselas*, which presents fictional examples of the truth of a formulable thesis (Sacks, p. 26). In *Sartor* Carlyle does proffer a set of ideas, but he chooses to move the reader by speaking to him through his fictions, rather than by engaging his interest in simple fictional narrative or the more sophisticated dramatic narrative of the novel. Like a novel, an apologue or exemplum depends on consistent narrative, on consistent representation of character and action, and on focusing the reader's attention on that narrative. Apologues and novels are forms of representation, while *Sartor* is a form of argument.[14] The nar-

---

[14] In discriminating *Sartor* from the novel, I have in mind Sheldon Sacks's definition of a novel or "action" as "a work organized

rative in *Sartor* is only apparent narrative, is not consistent, and does not gain our primary interest or embody Carlyle's primary intention. Any interest we take in it is carefully controlled by Carlyle's persuasive intention. Furthermore, *Sartor* refers to the actual world, rather than to the analogous, represented worlds of apologues and novels. As we read *Sartor*, we are aware we are reading something more like Burke's *Reflections on the Revolution in France* or the "Areopagitica" than like *Tom Jones* or *Great Expectations* or an apologue such as *Rasselas*.

Sartor is also not a work of "expression." Though the phrase is seldom defined, "work of expression" seems to mean a work that is determined largely by the character and mind of the author. In *The Mirror and the Lamp*, M. H. Abrams summarizes the "central tendency" of early nineteenth-century "expressive theory": "A work of art is essentially the internal made external, resulting from a creative process operating under the impulse of feeling, and embodying the combined product of the poet's perceptions, thoughts, and feelings."[15] This statement would apparently satisfy the critics in question as

so that it introduces characters about whose fates we are made to care, in unstable relationships which are then further complicated until the complication is finally resolved by the removal of the represented instability" (Sacks, p. 26). The crucial elements of my argument, however, are that the narrative of *Sartor* does not embody Carlyle's primary intention and that the reference of the book is to the actual.

[15] *The Mirror and the Lamp: Romantic Theory and the Critical Tradition* (New York: Oxford Univ. Press, 1953), p. 22. Cited in the text as Abrams. *Sartor* might better be described, within the categories outlined by Abrams, as a "pragmatic" work, and the view presented here as a "pragmatic theory" (Abrams, pp. 14–21).

a description of *Sartor*, or any work of "expression." To say that a work is expressive in this general sense tells us a great deal, but it does not tell us all we would like to know about the work's particular structure and coherence. We should like to know what "feeling" provided the necessary "impulse" and what relationship the writer's "perceptions, thoughts, and feelings" bear to each other and to the essential, impulsive feeling. Early nineteenth-century theoretical standards for works of expression were quite high and demanded a certain purity of motive or impulsive feeling. Abrams quotes Carlyle's friend John Stuart Mill, who says that when the poet's "act of utterance is not itself the end, but a means to an end,—viz., by the feelings he himself expresses, to work upon the feelings, or upon the belief or the will of another; when the expression of his emotions, or of his thoughts tinged by his emotions, is tinged also by that purpose, by that desire of making an impression upon another mind,—then it ceases to be poetry, and becomes eloquence" (Abrams, p. 22). By this standard, *Sartor* would certainly be called "eloquence." *Sartor* works on what Mill calls the "feelings," the "belief," and the "will" to change them and to promote action. This quality of *Sartor* distinguishes it from great works of expression like "Tintern Abbey," which is organized superbly to make the experience of the poet intelligible to the reader.[16] *Sartor* is not organized simply to make the reader under-

[16] See Robert Langbaum's *The Poetry of Experience: The Dramatic Monologue in Modern Literary Tradition* (London: Chatto and Windus, 1957), especially his introduction and first chapter, where he discusses *Sartor* and Wordsworth's poetry. Though I disagree with Langbaum's view of the motive behind *Sartor*, I am indebted to his book in many ways.

stand Carlyle's experience, what Mill calls his "perceptions, thoughts, and feelings." Instead, it uses Carlyle's
experience or a stylized version of it to persuade the
reader to believe in his ideas and act on them.[17]

The arrangement of the materials in *Sartor* is an ar-
gumentative or rhetorical order, not an explanatory or
simply logical order. The order is determined by argu-
mentative strategies and complicated by the use of fictions. The "development" of Carlyle's ideas—that is, the
sequential or organically progressive, intuitive, or logical
process that produces his set of ideas—may not always
be clear. Admittedly, the difficulty of tracing the process
of Carlyle's thought is due partly to the process itself.
Carlyle's thought depends on intuition and experience,
which are somewhat less orderly than logic. But it is not
Carlyle's purpose to reproduce this mental process in
clear steps for the reader. The ordering of his materials
depends on his intention to persuade, not to explain; and
in persuading, he must consider factors that do not nor-

[17] Elder Olson defines "expression" as "the *external* manifestation of activities and events in the mind that would otherwise remain private" in "The Lyric," *Poetic Theory/Poetic Practice*, ed.
Robert Scholes, Papers of the Midwest Modern Language Association Presented at the Annual Meeting for 1968, October 17, 18,
and 19, in Cincinnati, Ohio (Iowa City: Midwest Mod. Lang. Assn.,
1969), p. 62. In this sense, *Sartor* is not a work of expression. What
Carlyle has done instead is similar to what he insists a writer must
do who has an object belonging to "the invisible and immaterial
class," as opposed to the "material and visible" class: "He must
devise new means of explanation, describe conditions of mind in
which this invisible idea arises, the false persuasions that eclipse
it, the false shows that may be mistaken for it, the glimpses of it
that appear elsewhere; in short, strive, by a thousand well-devised
methods, to guide his reader up to the perception of it" ("State of
German Literature" [1827], *Works*, 26:71–72).

mally enter into explanation. He must control carefully his reader's feelings, anticipate objections, put down opposing points of view, in short, perform a variety of rhetorical maneuvers that may make his progress look "somewhat haphazard" to someone trying to determine the logical and intuitive structure that is the basis of Carlyle's view.

When Carlyle's thought is reduced to its essential logical and intuitive structure, it is often found wanting. John H. Muirhead, for example, in *The Platonic Tradition in Anglo-Saxon Philosophy*, states the following objection to Carlyle as a philosopher:

If, as he himself held, the construction of "an intellectual scheme or ground-plan of the universe with one's own instruments" was indespensable [sic] to the thinker, how, in the absence of it, could there be any security in his work against gaps and misfits, joists at one place without support, at another running counter to one another? To say that Carlyle's building was a patchwork of this kind would be wholly untrue. What is undeniable is that a matter so fundamental could not with impunity be neglected and that no literary brilliancy could make up for the want of firmly drawn, consistently developed philosophical principles. In the result his contempt of "Metaphysic" took its revenge, on the one hand by surrounding his central teaching with an air of unsubstantiality, which made it an easy prey to cold positivist analysis, on the other in an exaggeration of half-truths, which went far to vitiate the effect of what was truest in it.[18]

This criticism is sound and yet inadequate to the experience of reading *Sartor*. Carlyle's ideas are perplexing and the mind struggles in the effort to systematize them.

[18] "Carlyle's Transcendental Symbolism," in *The Platonic Tradition* (London: G. Allen and Unwin, 1931), p. 141.

But fortunately the power of *Sartor* does not rest solely on the power of Carlyle's ideas. It depends in large part on those ideas as they are stated in a complex rhetorical arrangement and on their statement through fictions. The fictions increase the complexity of the book, to the further puzzlement of "cold positivist analysis," and if we have patience, they increase our pleasure. *Sartor* will disappoint those seeking clear, explanatory statement of ideas; and it will frustrate, as it often does, lovers of fable or narrative fiction by the directness with which it speaks. If one takes it as it is, a complex persuasion operating in and through fictions, its power will be found to be strong.

The need for fictions and for the kinds of rhetoric they allow may seem to arise directly from Carlyle's epistemology. Carlyle's rhetoric is not based on a logical proof. Nor is it based on inspiration, though Carlyle would want us sometimes to believe that it is. In *Sartor* Carlyle uses what can be called rhetoric of the imagination.[19] His arguments are based on what Carlyle calls intuition quickened by experience. Premises based on what is known imaginatively or intuitively and supported by one's immediate, felt experience in the world demand different kinds of arguments and different modes of speech, a new rhetoric.

The kind of heightened, fictionalized persuasive statement Carlyle's ideas are given in *Sartor* is not, however, determined absolutely by the nature of Carlyle's ideas

---

[19] Mark Roberts suggests another phrase, the "rhetoric of unreason," in "Carlyle and the Rhetoric of Unreason," *EIC*, 18 (1968), 397–419. Roberts sees the function of aspects of Carlyle's rhetoric in *Sartor* and *Past and Present*, but he is suspicious of their effects.

or of his mode of arriving at them. *Sartor* is not the necessary form of "expression" of his ideas, even though such may at times seem the case. The full outlines of the Clothes Philosophy can be found in Carlyle's early essays, without the elaborate devices of statement found in *Sartor*. Carlyle exercised choices in the creation of this unusual book, choices guided not simply by the nature of his ideas but by his desire to state them in a persuasive and moving way.

Sartor is, then, not a novel, not a work designed simply to reveal the character and thought of its author, and not a philosophical demonstration or expository essay. *Sartor* is a complex persuasive essay that operates in and through fictions. It is not a form of representation but a form of speaking, a form of speaking to move others to belief and action. It is, further, an agonistic mode of speaking, especially in its use of fictional devices, designed to delight and amaze, while it moves one to belief.

2: The Invention of
Sartor Resartus

I *have* a Book in me that will cause ears
to tingle; and one day out it must and will
issue.

CARLYLE TO JOHN CARLYLE[1]

CARLYLE'S intentions in writing *Sartor*, as he revealed
them in his notebooks and letters, were to speak the
truth about the nature of the world and to stir the English
nation to action. As he wrote the book, he was uncertain
about the effectiveness of the unusual form of speaking
he had chosen, but his intentions never wavered. Although he once called *Sartor* "a kind of Didactic Novel,"
the letter to James Fraser in which he did so was written
with special diplomacy after many unsuccessful attempts
to get *Sartor* published; and it is not strange that he
should be drawn to a conventional term to name his un-
conventional book. He saw *Sartor* as an attempt to persuade, not to delight and instruct by means of a dramatic
narrative or to reveal himself.

When Carlyle began writing *Sartor*, he wished to write
a book. For him a book represented something original,
not a review or history of someone else's work, something
independent of the periodicals in which he had been
forced to do most of his work, and something that would

[1] 19 December 1830 (*Letters*, 1:242).

allow him to preach the truth he felt he knew. He began
Sartor as an essay for a periodical, and he did not see it
at first as the book he wished to write. Carlyle began
Sartor late in the summer of 1830. He was living in isolation with his wife Jane, his brother Alick, and Alick's
wife and their households, at Craigenputtock in Dum-
friesshire, Scotland.[2] He had gone there from Edinburgh
in 1828 to live cheaply and to free himself from the necessity of doing hack work. He wanted by the summer of
1830 to write a book, but he was restricted by want of
money, by the lack of a fit subject, and by his knowledge
that he would have trouble getting a book published. He
was tired of writing book reviews, even though he had
learned to manipulate that form to his own persuasive
ends,[3] and he was weary of the German authors who had
occupied so much of his time for the previous ten years.
In late August 1830 he told Goethe that once his present
work, his *History of German Literature*, was put aside,
"I must forthwith betake me to something more con-
genial and original: except writing from the heart and if
possible to the heart, Life has no other business for me,
no other pleasure."[4] A few months before, while working on his *History*, he had written in his notebook that
he was almost done with the Germans: "Having seized

---

[2] See the description of the farm in Neff, pp. 97–101.

[3] His review essays were so very much original that, as G. B.
Tennyson says, we tend to forget that all of his early essays were
in fact reviews (*Sartor Called Resartus*, p. 84). In June 1828 Carlyle had remarked to his brother John about Lockhart's *Life of
Burns*, the subject of his essay "Burns": "It is this Book (a trivial
enough one) which I am to *pretend* reviewing" (*Letters*, 1:157–58).

[4] *Correspondence Between Goethe and Carlyle*, ed. Charles Eliot
Norton (London: Macmillan, 1887), p. 210.

their opinions, I must turn me to inquire *how* true are they? That truth is in them, no lover of Truth will doubt: but how much? And after all, one needs an intellectual Scheme (or ground plan of the Universe) drawn with one's own instruments."[5]

In December 1829 he had told John Wilson, "I have some thoughts of beginning to *prophesy* next year, if I prosper; that seems the best style, could one strike it rightly."[6] But the proper style and mode for prophesying were not ready at hand. Earlier that year, in January, he mourned for a time of more complete freedom: "Alas for the days when Diogenes could fit up his tub, and let the 'literary world' and all other worlds, except the only true one within his own soul wag hither and thither at discretion!" (*Letters*, 1:188). The present was not free, and Carlyle was at some loss to find the proper manner in which to speak. In the letter to Goethe quoted above, he went on to say, "When I look at the wonderful Chaos within me, full of natural Supernaturalism, and all manner of Antediluvian fragments; and how the Universe is daily growing more mysterious as well as more august, and the influences from without more heterogeneous and perplexing; I see not well what is to come of it all, and only conjecture from the violence of the fermentation that something strange may come."

By late August 1830 Carlyle was preoccupied with his own ideas. He had a powerful desire to speak out, but he

[5] *Two Note Books of Thomas Carlyle from 23d March 1822 to 16th May 1832*, ed. Charles Eliot Norton (New York: Grolier Club, 1898), pp. 150–51. Cited in the text as *TN*.

[6] Quoted in Mary Gordon, *"Christopher North": A Memoir of John Wilson* (New York: W. J. Widdleton, 1870), p. 323.

did not see how to do so. He could only predict that he
would produce something "strange." His commitment to
writing an original work was strengthened by the failure
of his *History of German Literature*. Public enthusiasm
for German subjects had waned, and he had been driven
to project organizing his book into review articles "and
so realizing *something* for my Year's work." On September 7 he found this venture would not succeed, and
he wrote, "The 'Course of Providence' (nay sometimes I
almost feel that there *is* such a thing even for *me*) seems
guiding my steps into new regions; the question is coming more and more towards a decision: Canst thou, there
as thou art, accomplish aught good and true, or art thou
to die miserably as a vain Pretender?" (*TN*, p. 163).
Carlyle's desire to produce something "good and true"
was strong indeed.[7] Although he did not at first see a
piece that began as an essay on Clothes as the original
book he wanted to write, his awareness that it could be
a pulpit from which he could speak to the nation grew
as he wrote.

Carlyle's first recorded remark about *Sartor* is in his

[7] Carlyle's desire to speak in an original and timely form was
due partly to certain truths he found as a critic of other writers. In
"State of German Literature," written in the early fall of 1827
(dated in *Sartor Called Resartus*, p. 336), he said, "Among the
deadliest of poetical sins is imitation; for if every man must have
his own way of thought, and his own way of expressing it, much
more every nation" (*Works*, 26:70). In "Goethe's Helena," written
in early 1828 (dated in *Sartor Called Resartus*, p. 336), Carlyle
wrote, "If an artist has conceived his subject in the secret shrine of
his own mind, and knows, with a knowledge beyond all power of
cavil, that it is true and pure, he may choose his own manner of
exhibiting it, and will generally be the fittest to choose it as well"
(*Works*, 26:149).

notebook: "I am going to write—Nonsense. It is on 'Clothes.' Heaven be my Comforter!" (*TN*, p. 176). After six weeks he comments, "Written a strange piece 'On Clothes': know not what will come of it. October 28.th 1830" (*TN*, p. 177). During this interval he made several references to this "strange piece" in his letters. After writing for three weeks, he considered that the work might become "a Book or a string of Magazine Articles; we hope the former; but in either case it might be worth something" (*Letters*, 1:235). He remained uncertain about exactly how to characterize his work and about its potential effectiveness. On 19 October he wrote to John Carlyle, his brother, "What I am writing at is the strangest of all things: begun as an Article for *Fraser*; then found to be too long (except it were divided into two); now sometimes looking almost as if it would swell into a Book. A very singular piece, I assure you! It glances from Heaven to Earth and back again in a strange satirical frenzy, whether fine or not remains to be seen. . . . *Teufelsdreck* (that is the title of my present *Schrift*) will be done (so far—fifty pages) tomorrow. . . ." (*Letters*, 1:237). His remarks emphasize the uniqueness and oddity of the work, but it is at least clear that he did not regard it as a novel. He says that it began as an "Article" and calls it his "*Schrift*," a "piece." None of these is a name a novelist would apply to his story in its early stages. Yet, since he calls it *Teufelsdreck*, the article must have contained his primary fiction from the very first. In his letters and other recorded remarks, he refers to it consistently throughout its composition as his "book," his "manuscript," or as "Teufelsdreck," and, at least in his published letters and notebooks, he calls it a "novel" only once, in special circumstances.

Carlyle regarded *Fraser's Magazine*, the periodical he had in mind in the early stages of writing, in a special light. Its tone and manner did not seem wholly respectable to him, but he felt that its rhetoric was especially adapted to the times. The first number of *Fraser's* had appeared in February 1830.[8] In early September Carlyle had received "a whole Bundle of Fraser Magazines," which contained his own "Jean Paul Friedrich Richter's Review of Madame de Stael's 'Allemagne' " (*Fraser's*, 1 [1830], 28–37, 407–13) and two of his brother's "little Papers" (*TN*, pp. 170–71). He read over this new magazine and wrote in his notebook: "This out-Blackwoods Blackwood. Nevertheless the thing has its meaning: a kind of wild popular Lower-Comedy; of which John Wilson is the Inventor: It may perhaps, for it seems well adapted to the age, carry down his name to other times, as his most remarkable achievement." *Fraser's* wildness attracted and repelled him, but it was "well adapted to the age," and, Carlyle adds, "All the Magazines (except the New Monthly) seem to aim at it: a certain quickness, fluency of banter, not excluding sharp insight, and

[8] On *Fraser's* and related magazines see R. G. Cox, "The Great Reviews," *Scrutiny*, 6 (1937), 2–20, 155–70; Miriam Mulford Hunt Thrall, *Rebellious Fraser's: Nol Yorke's Magazine in the Days of Maginn, Thackeray, and Carlyle* (New York: Columbia Univ. Press, 1934); and Michael Allen, *Poe and the British Magazine Tradition* (New York: Oxford Univ. Press, 1969). Allen's extremely well-informed book is a great help in understanding the context in which Carlyle operated when he began *Sartor* as an article for *Fraser's*.

Merry-Andrew Drollery, and even Humor, are available here; however, the grand requisite seems to be Impudence, and a fearless committing of yourself to talk in your Drink.—*Literature* has nothing to do with this, but Printing has; and Printing is now no more the peculiar symbol and livery of Literature than writing was in Gutenberg's day." Such rhetoric may have seemed subliterary, but something employing it could be printed and would be adapted to the age.

Fraser's and the magazines Carlyle associated with it offered him playful and varied rhetoric. They also offered fictional voices. The use of fictional editors, commentators, and narrators to perform a variety of rhetorical functions was a highly developed convention in *Blackwood's*, the magazine on which *Fraser's* was modeled, and in *Fraser's* itself. In the early numbers of *Fraser's* that Carlyle had received, fictional voices introduce stories of the supernatural ironically in order to make them acceptable to a scientific, modern age,[9] satirize and parody writers under review,[10] ridicule contemporary figures,[11] provide an editorial voice for the magazine.[12] Carlyle himself adapted similar voices to his own uses between the beginning of *Sartor* and its publication. His "Four

[9] See "Remarkable Vision of Charles XI. of Sweden," *Fraser's*, 1 (1830), 120–25.

[10] See "Poetry of the Magyars," *Fraser's*, 1 (1830), 155–77; "The Magyars *versus* Dr. Bowring," 1:433–42; "Whewell's Notation of Political Economy: A Fragment," 1:303–08.

[11] See "The Election of Editor for Fraser's Magazine," *Fraser's*, 1 (1830), 496–508, 738–757; "A Gossip about Arts and Artists," 1:533–40; "Poems to Distinguished Individuals," 1:711–13.

[12] See "Oliver Yorke's" reply to "Letter from a Tory from Principle, Not Prejudice. To Oliver Yorke, Esq.," *Fraser's*, 2 (1830–31), 89–92.

Fables" were published in *Fraser's* (2 [1830–31], 178–79; *Works*, 26:471–72) and were signed "Pilpay Junior." "Sauerteig" made his appearance in *Fraser's* in Carlyle's "Biography" and "Count Cagliostro" (*Works*, 28:44–61, 249–318) and "Smelfungus Redivivus" appeared in the *Edinburgh Review* in his "Corn-Law Rhymes" (*Works*, 28:136–66). Teufelsdröckh made his first public appearances in *Fraser's* in "The Tale" (*Works*, 27:447–79) and "On History Again" (*Works*, 28:167–76) as "D. T." and under his full name in the *Foreign Quarterly Review* in "Goethe's Works" (*Works*, 27:385–443). It is important for our understanding of *Sartor* to note that Carlyle associated such fictional devices with periodical essays and used them in such essays himself. The very appearance of Teufelsdröckh in the magazines is an indication that he is a rhetorical device suitable to essay writing, something different from a character in a novel and from a device for self-revelation. Thus *Fraser's*, as a vehicle, offered Carlyle the use of fictional voices and the use of a complex variety of tones—playful, satirical, serious, hyperbolic—offered, in short, what seemed effective rhetorical methods and a channel to the English public.

In the essay Carlyle began for *Fraser's* he made important choices. He took an original subject, "Clothes," and wrote his own essay, rather than a review of someone else's work. He also took advantage of the kinds of rhetoric and rhetorical devices he found in *Fraser's*. His descriptions of his unusual essay are consistent with his descriptions of what he found in the magazine. Furthermore, he invented the fictional voice of "Teufelsdreck" and probably of the Editor. At a minimum Carlyle would need a fictional Editor to introduce the work on

"Clothes," by Teufelsdreck, just as he uses "O. Y."
(Oliver Yorke) to introduce "On History Again," by one
"assiduous 'D. T.' " (Diogenes Teufelsdröckh) (*Works*,
28:167). Oliver Yorke himself, just elected editor in
July 1830 (*Fraser's*, 1:496–508, 738–57), and other fic-
tional spokesmen in *Fraser's* were available as models.
Christopher North and his cronies were available in
Blackwood's.

Before 12 November 1830, when he informed John
Carlyle that he had done so, he sent this piece of fifty
pages or so to William Fraser. He wrote in his notebook,
"Sent away the *Clothes*; of which I could make a kind of
Book; but cannot *afford* it. Have still *the* Book *in petto* (?)
but in the most chaotic shape" (*TN*, p. 178). Financial
pressures and other circumstances at first kept Carlyle
from writing the book he had "*in petto*," but he did wish
to develop at greater length the arguments he had begun.
He wavered between a book and a set of articles as a
means of doing so. On 12 November he told John that he
had sent William Fraser "that *Teufelsdreck* paper of
mine, which I have now resolved not to make a Book
of; but, if I have opportunity, two *Articles*, and the germ
of more" (*Letters*, 1:238).[13]

Fraser, however, delayed the manuscript, and Carlyle
changed his mind. On 21 January 1831 he wrote to John
telling him to get the article back. Carlyle's instructions

[13] The practice of dividing articles seems to have been rather
arbitrary, as was the dividing of *Sartor* for *Fraser's* in 1833. Struc-
turally, the article on "Clothes" would be unlikely to vary whether
it was printed as one article or two. The articles published in successive numbers of *Fraser's* in 1832 as "Biography" and "Boswell's
Life of Johnson" were in fact one essay split for publication (*TN*,
p. 255).

are stated with special vehemence, fed in the context of
the letter by outrage at the magazine's financial policies
and its general tone: "Certainly that *Fraser's Magazine*
gives the most scurvy remuneration of any Periodical extant, and shall have no more stuff of mine at that rate,
barring worse fortune than I have yet seen. . . . It is also
a frothy, washy, punchy, dirty kind of Periodical, I fear."
Accordingly, he asked John to "go to Fraser and get from
him by all means my long Paper entitled *Thoughts on
Clothes*: I would not for above half a dozen reasons have
it appear there so long as I have potatoes to eat." In addition to these reasons, Carlyle says, "I have taken a notion that I can make rather a good *Book*, and one, above
all, likely to produce some desirable impression on the
world even now." He asked John to read it critically and
added, "I can devise some more biography for *Teufelsdreck*; give a second deeper part, in the same vein, leading through Religion and the nature of Society, and Lord
knows what." The "Thoughts," he felt, "slightly altered,
would itself make a little volume first (which would encourage me immensely) could one find any Bookseller,
which however I suppose one cannot." He urged John to
show the piece to Fraser and to Edward Irving and con-
cluded, "I fear perfect *anonymity* is now out of the question; however swear everyone to secrecy, for I mean to
speak fearlessly if at all" (*Letters*, 1:248–50).

This letter tells us more about the choices Carlyle
made in writing *Sartor*. It emphasizes again his dissatis-
faction with periodicals, especially *Fraser's*, as a platform
and his desire to speak independently through an extended work of his own. It shows us explicitly Carlyle's
purpose of producing "some desirable impression on the

world even now," which became even more pronounced as *Sartor* progressed. His desire for anonymity and for a means of speaking "fearlessly" helps to explain his use of fictions. The way in which he speaks of the growth of the book suggests that it will not grow as a work of narrative fiction would. He will add, significantly, more "biography" and apparently extend his argument "through Religion and the nature of Society" and more.[14]

In January 1831 Carlyle had decided to make his article into a book according to a fairly definite plan. The making of *Sartor*, however, was not easy. Froude, who wanted to make a virtue of haste, claimed the work grew as "fast as he could throw his ideas upon paper."[15] In fact, Carlyle worked hard on the book, overcoming his own doubts about its quality as he labored. In early February 1831 he wrote in his notebook that he had asked John "to liberate my *Teufelsdreck* from Editorial durance

---

[14] The traditional view of the relationship of "Thoughts on Clothes" to *Sartor* is that the article went into Book First of *Sartor*, the "more biography for Teufelsdreck" became Book Second, and "the second deeper part, in the same vein, leading through Religion and the nature of Society, and Lord knows what" became Book Third. See Harrold, *Sartor*, p. xxv; *Sartor Called Resartus*, p. 142. See also Tennyson's answer to S. B. Liljegren's theory that *Sartor* began as the chapter on "The Dandiacal Body" in *Sartor Called Resartus*, pp. 132–33. The traditional view seems reasonable, but since the composition of *Sartor* was painstaking, it is unlikely, in fact impossible, that Book First as it stands now represents the original "Thoughts on Clothes." For evidence of the kind of care Carlyle was capable of taking in his writing, see Grace J. Calder's *The Writing of Past and Present: A Study of Carlyle's Manuscripts*, Yale Studies in English, 112 (New Haven: Yale Univ. Press, 1949).

[15] *Thomas Carlyle: A History of the First Forty Years of His Life, 1795–1835*, II, 104.

in London, and am seriously thinking to make a Book of it." He was not satisfied with it but was committed to making something of it: "The thing is not right, not *Art*; yet perhaps a nearer approach to Art than I have yet made. We ought to try" (*TN*, p. 183). Carlyle worked diligently on *Sartor* through the spring of 1831, planning ultimately to complete it in July in order to take it to London in hope of finding a publisher. His comments on the book in the spring and early summer reflect his purpose of speaking to the world and, at the same time, his continuing doubts about his ability to do so in the particular, unique form he had chosen. He wrote to John on 6 June 1831 that he was busy with *Sartor* and that "it will be one of the strangest volumes ever offered to the English world, whether *worth* anything is another question" (*Letters*, 1:289–90). In spite of all the obstacles before him, the work was to be "offered to the English world." Carlyle aspired to a wide audience for his oratory, necessarily, since it was "the English world" he was trying to direct on a proper course. He was still pressed financially, but he did his task with care: "Here I am writing most *deliberately* for the last six months; and I know not in the least whether I shall ever gain the price of my paper" (*Letters*, 1:291).[16]

The writing was difficult and his attitude toward the quality of his work wavered, but his intention was clear. On 12 July he wrote to John, "I am struggling forward

[16] Most of his writing in this spring and early summer of 1831 was on *Sartor*. In January he wrote three reviews, "Taylor's Historic Survey of German Poetry," "The Nibelungen Lied," and "Early German Literature" and probably one poem (*Sartor Called Resartus*, pp. 337–38). The three review essays came out of his *History of German Literature*.

with *Dreck*, sick enough, but not in bad heart. I think the world will nowise be enraptured with this (medicinal) *Devil's Dung*; that the critical republic will cackle vituperatively or perhaps maintain total silence: *à la bonne heure!* It was the best I had in me; what God had given me, what the Devil shall not take away" (*Letters*, 1:299). The "desirable impression" he hoped to produce on the world was medicinal. Carlyle felt a religious purpose and would not compromise with the "critical republic." He left Craigenputtock for London at last on 4 August 1831, with his manuscript. In the city he found the need for his medicinal book at least as great as he had imagined. In August 1831, after his first unsuccessful bout with London publishers, he wrote to his wife at Craigenputtock, "That is the temper in which I find many here: they deplore the prevalence of dishonesty, quackery and stupidity; many do it . . . with apparent heartiness and sorrow: but to believe that it can be *resisted*, that it will and shall be resisted, herein poor *Teufelsdreck* is well-nigh singular" (*Letters*, 1:319). The book was intended to do moral combat, but was held from the fray by the Reform Bill which slowed publishing to a standstill.[17] Carlyle's book was by 10 October assigned to a box for safekeeping. On that date he reflected on the failure of the Reform Bill two days before and on what he should do:

Meanwhile *what* were the true duty of a man; were it to stand utterly aloof from Politics (not ephemeral only, for that

[17] See *Letters*, pp. 254, 259; *Sartor Called Resartus*, p. 147; *The Letters of Thomas Carlyle to His Brother Alexander*, ed. Edwin W. Marrs, Jr. (Cambridge, Mass.: Belknap Press of Harvard Univ. Press, 1968), pp. 276, 277, 279, 295, 298. This last volume will be cited as *Letters to Alexander*.

of course, but generally from all speculation about social systems &c. &c.); or is not perhaps the very want of this time, an infinite want of Governors, of Knowledge how to govern itself?—Canst *thou* in any measure spread abroad Reverence over the hearts of men? That were a far higher task than *any* other. Is it to be done by Art; or are men's minds as yet shut to Art, and open only at best to oratory; not fit for a *Meister*, but only for a better and better *Teufelsdreck; Denk' und schweig!*

[TN, pp. 203–04]

Carlyle saw his book as a form of oratory, distinct from the novelistic form of *Wilhelm Meister*, directed to the needs of his time and adapted to its special demands. His purpose is serious. He does not wish to entertain or amuse, but to work fundamental reform, to produce by his oratory an attitude that will direct the conduct of the nation.

The book he had created in the spring and early summer of 1831 was a complex persuasive essay designed to speak to Englishmen about the state of their nation and of their very souls. Carlyle strove to give them new hope, a new sense of themselves, and knowledge how to govern themselves, and tried to "spread abroad Reverence over the hearts of men" (*TN*, p. 203). He did so through fictions that allowed him to speak fearlessly yet truthfully and in a conciliatory and therefore maximally persuasive manner. He must have been pleased with his choice of form when his brother John wrote from London on 9 June 1831, as he was finishing *Sartor*, that Carlyle needed only to find his "place among men in order to exercise more influence on the present age than any living writer." John reported that the "little fragments" Carlyle had published "show an extent of knowledge, a

keenness and depth of insight, a clear and fearless liberty
that I find in no English writer of these times." John is
certain that his brother "will meet response from many
hearts even in these times of Mammon." The faithful
John has, however, one criticism, which in view of the
form of *Sartor* must have pleased Carlyle most: "The
only fault, if it may be so named, of your writing is that
it is too high and sustained for almost all English readers.
There are few who can bear to have so much intense and
continued thought put upon them as any of your papers
require. The fault I think rises almost entirely from your
isolation and consequent want of knowledge of the audience you have to address. You fire well and stoutly, but
have to take aim in the twilight, and can never rightly
discern whether you have hit or missed the mark" (Neff,
pp. 121–22).

This time Carlyle's thought was in more palatable and,
hopefully, more effective form, but not so palatable that
it sacrificed truthfulness. John's metaphor of the cannon
is apt. Carlyle was not fundamentally a timid man. In the
midst of seeking a publisher, on 14 January 1832, he
wrote to Alexander, "With incessant long-continued ex-
ertion, there is *much* possible for me; I may become a
Preacher of the Truth, and so deliver my message in this
Earth, the highest that can be entrusted to man" (*Letters
to Alexander*, pp. 299–300). He could be conciliatory and
amusing instead of intense and thoughtful, but not at the
expense of truth. *Sartor* too was fired off into the twilight, a shell of new design, improved by hints sent back
from the field.

The story of Carlyle's difficulties in getting *Sartor* published, "the beggarly history of poor *Sartor among the*

Blockheadisms," [18] has been told many times, most recently by G. B. Tennyson (*Sartor Called Resartus*, pp.
146–55). It is a story of continuous frustration which finally brought Carlyle and his manuscript in 1833 back to
Fraser's, where he began and where he wanted less and
less to be. One of his purposes in writing *Sartor* was to
get free of periodicals, but he did not succeed until Emerson published *Sartor* in America in 1836 and Carlyle
himself followed with an English edition in 1838.[19] Between 1831 and 1833, when *Sartor* appeared in *Fraser's*,
Carlyle saw more and more acutely the world's need for
his book, while publisher after publisher refused to accept it. The world here, he wrote to Goethe from London
in August 1831, "is dancing a Tarantula Dance of Political Reform, and has no ear left for Literature. Nevertheless, I shall do my utmost to get the work, which was
meant to be a 'word spoken in season,' actually emit-
ted."[20] If he could not get his word published, and it
became more apparent daily that he could not, he knew
he had done his best, though he was often discouraged.
By 10 October, having assigned *Teufelsdreck* to a box
for safekeeping, at least temporarily, he wrote in his notebook, "There must he continue, till the Book-trade revive
a little; yet perhaps there is material in it: in any case I

[18] Carlyle's phrase, *Reminiscences by Thomas Carlyle*, ed.
Charles Eliot Norton (London: Macmillan, 1887), 1:91.

[19] Isaac Watson Dyer, *A Bibliography of Thomas Carlyle's
Writings and Ana* (Portland, Me.: Southworth Press, 1928), pp.
220–23. Cited hereafter as Dyer.

[20] *Correspondence Between Goethe and Carlyle*, p. 290. Carlyle's quotation is from Isaiah 50:4: "The Lord God hath given me
the tongue of the learned, that I should know how to speak a word
in season to him that is weary."

did my best" (*TN*, p. 201).[21] On 16 October he com-
plained to Mill about his inability to publish books and
his need to resort to the "monstrous method" of putting
his books into periodicals. Until there is a proper "Periodical Pulpit," from which the Philistines are excluded,
one must "Speak! Preach! The Night cometh. Where men
are, there is an audience: 'You may make a Pulpit by
inverting any Tub!' To such strange shifts are we reduced."[22] The audience was there. Diogenes Teufelsdröckh with his Tub and his Editor was ready, but he
could not speak.

The manuscript was in and out of its box for several
months. The publisher Murray returned it "with a polite
enough note, and a 'Criticism' from some altogether im-
mortal 'master of German Literature,' to me quite unknown; which Criticism (a miserable, Dandiacal *quodli-
bet*, in the usual vein) did *not* authorise the Publication
in these times" (*Letters*, 1:357). This criticism, which
Carlyle printed in the first London edition of *Sartor*
(Dyer, p. 223),[23] was not likely to increase Carlyle's confidence in his work. It said in part, "The Author of *Teufelsdröckh* is a person of talent; his work displays here
and there some felicity of thought and expression, considerable fancy and knowledge: but whether or not it

[21] He made similar remarks about the book trade and having to
lock up his "Poor Bundle of Papers" to William Graham seven
days later. See *Letters of Thomas Carlyle to William Graham*, ed.
John Graham, Jr. (Princeton: Princeton Univ. Press, 1950), p. 56.

[22] *Letters of Thomas Carlyle to John Stuart Mill, John Sterling,
and Robert Browning*, ed. Alexander Carlyle (New York: Frederick A. Stokes Co., 1923), p. 21. This volume will be cited as *Letters to Mill*.

[23] Harrold reprints it in *Sartor*, p. 319.

would take with the public seems doubtful. For a *jeu d'esprit* of that kind it is too long; it would have suited better as an essay or article than as a volume" (*Sartor*, p. 319). The irony of a "Bookseller's Taster" telling him to make an article out of his labors must have been unbearable. It is significant for the matter of classification that the Taster, like other early reviewers and readers, does not mistake the book for a novel.

While *Sartor* was challenged on the publisher's front, it gained ground on others. William Glen read it " 'with infinite satisfaction;' John Mill with fears that 'the world would take some time to see what meaning was in it.' "[24] In January 1832 he had given it to his former pupil Charles Buller, and he wrote to John Carlyle, "My chief comfort is in the effect it appears to produce on young *unbestimmt* people like him: Glen was even asking for a *third* perusal of it. The whole matter is none of the weightiest: yet also is it not wholly a Lie that Lucubration of Dreck's; it can rest for twelvemonths and will not worm-eat" (*Letters*, 1:391). The book did rest until late in the spring of 1833 when he wrote to John that he would cut his book up for *Fraser's*, that he could get some money for it and at least get it published, "which otherwise there is little hope of, to *any* purpose or without great loss; the Book-trade being still dead,—and as I reckon forever" (*Letters*, 2:99–100). It could not have been easy for Carlyle to approach "the infatuated Fraser, with his Dog's-meat cart of a magazine" (*TN*, p. 232). When he wrote John in January 1832 about throwing an

[24] Carlyle in a letter to John Carlyle, quoted by Froude in *Thomas Carlyle: A History of the First Forty Years of His Life, 1795–1835*, II, 198.

essay on Dr. Johnson onto Fraser's cart, he consoled himself with the thought that "each age has its capabilities; these are the capabilities of ours" (*Letters*, 1:389).

Necessity forced Carlyle to approach *Fraser's* again. On 17 May 1833 he wrote to John, "My chief project for the summer is to cut Teufelsdreck into slips, and have it printed in *Fraser's Magazine*: I have not proposed it to him yet, and must go warily to work in that, for I have spoiled such things already by want of diplomacy" (*Letters*, 2:99). The book was back where it had started, although it was not reduced to a mere article. The famous letter to James Fraser is conciliatory but, as always, honest. Carlyle recalls to Fraser's attention the "Manuscript *Book*," emphasizing its true nature, which he had brought to London and failed to strike any bargain for, "during that Reform hurly-burly, which unluckily still continues and is like to continue." Carlyle says that he has decided at last "to slit it up into strips, and send it forth in the Periodical way; for which in any case it was perhaps better adapted." But Carlyle cannot give it up to the periodical way easily: "The pains I took with the composition of it, truly, were greater than even I might have thought necessary, had this been foreseen: but what then? Care of that sort is never altogether thrown away; far better too much than too little." Carlyle insists that *Fraser's* is the first magazine he thinks of for publishing his book and that especially the "Conservative (though Anti-quack)" Editor would "suit *Fraser* perhaps better than any other Magazine." This was certainly true, though Carlyle disliked the magazine.

Carlyle describes his manuscript, labeling it tentatively as a novel. In the context of the letter and of Carlyle's other comments about his book, the claim that the book is a novel or that Carlyle thought it was looks rather weak. He told Fraser:

It is put together in the fashion of a kind of Didactic Novel: but indeed properly *like* nothing yet extant: I used to characterise it briefly as a kind of "Satirical Extravaganza on Things in General"; it contains more of my opinions on Art, Politics, Religion, Heaven, Earth and Air, than all the things I have yet written. The Creed promulgated on all these things, as you may judge, is *mine*, and firmly *believed*: for the rest, the main Actor in the business ("Editor of these Sheets," as he often calls himself) assumes a kind of Conservative (though Anti-quack) character; and would suit *Fraser* perhaps better than any other Magazine. The ultimate result, however, I need hardly premise, is a deep religious speculative-radicalism (so I call it for want of a better name), with which you are already well enough acquainted in me.

[*Letters*, 2:103–06]

Carlyle's emphasis is on "the Creed promulgated on all these things" and "the ultimate result." His intent to spread this creed, which "is *mine*, and firmly *believed*," is what gives unity to *Sartor* and determines what it is, a unique form of persuasive essay, suited to his own ideas and to the particular needs and demands of his audience, as he understood them. Carlyle's subsequent description of those who have read the book gives further evidence of this persuasive intention: "There are only five persons that have yet read this Manuscript: of whom two have expressed themselves (I mean convinced me that they *are*) considerably interested and gratified; two quite *struck*, 'overwhelmed with astonishment and new hope' (this is the result I aimed at for souls worthy of hope); and one in secret discontented and displeased" (*Letters*,

2:106). Carlyle aims not at telling a story, not at reveal-
ing himself so he may be understood and appreciated,
and not at outlining his ideas clearly and logically. He
aims at propagating a creed in such a way that it will
have a specific emotional effect, "astonishment and new
hope."

Carlyle knew full well the mixed response the work
would create among critics, but at no time during the
composition of *Sartor* does he indicate a willingness to
permit his intention to persuade the people of the truth
to be compromised by any effort to please the critics. He
told Fraser, "My own conjecture is that *Teufelsdröckh*,
whenever published, will astonish most that read it, be
wholly understood by very few; but to the astonishment
of some will add touches of (almost the deepest) spiritual
interest, with others quite the opposite feeling. I think I
can practically prophesy that for some six or eight
months (for it must be published without interruption),
it would be apt at least to *keep the eyes* of the Public on
you." Concluding his plea, he remarks, "Let me hear as
soon as you can; for the time seems come to set these
little bits of Doctrine forth" (*Letters*, 2:106–07).

Sartor was divided up, apparently a certain amount of
introductory material was added, and a few other
changes were made.[25] The emendations were not suffi-

[25] G. B. Tennyson notes that the title was emended between the
book's completion in 1831 and its publication in February 1833
(*Sartor Called Resartus*, p. 152). Since "Teufelsdreck" meant,
among other things (see *Sartor Called Resartus*, pp. 28n, 205, 220–
22 for explications of the name), asafoetida, the change in name
would make this "(medicinal) *Devil's Dung*" easier to swallow.
There were other emendations as well. The title was changed from
"Thoughts on Clothes; or Life and Opinions of Herr D. Teufels-

cient, however, to make *Sartor* really suitable to *Fraser's*
and its readers. As Carlyle predicted at the end of the
book, it brought down the wrath of its readers on the
publisher. It was vilified as it appeared in *Fraser's* from
November 1833 to August 1834, excluding January and

---

dröckh, D.U.J." to *Sartor Resartus* for *Fraser's*, then to *Sartor Resartus: The Life and Opinions of Herr Teufelsdröckh* for the 1838 London edition of *Sartor* (Dyer, pp. 220, 223). He had told James Fraser the title might be altered a little, and he apparently invented the new one to suit the tone both of his piece and of *Fraser's*. He wrote Mill on 18 July 1833: "*Teufelsdröckh*, under the as whimsical title of *Sartor Resartus*, is to come out piecemeal in *Fraser's Magazine*" (*Letters to Mill*, p. 64). The piece may have been better suited to *Fraser's* than any other magazine, but changes other than in the title were needed. On 25 June 1833 he had written to his mother: "Fraser I believe *is* to have my Manuscript Book; which will therefore require a very little sorting: but on the whole I prefer resting for a while" (*Letters*, 2:109). He had also told Fraser that "some brief Introduction could fit it handsomely enough into its new destination" and that it would "want the Introduction, and various other 'O. Y.'s' that will perhaps be useful" (*Letters*, 2:105, 107). The changes were probably made in the period of comparative quiet of late June and early July 1833, before the letter to Mill giving the change in title and speaking of a definite agreement with Fraser. Carlyle must have added at this time certain references to *Fraser's* in the text, to make the work fit the magazine. It is unlikely that these references survived from the first version of *Sartor*, since it was withdrawn for revision and expansion so emphatically. It is also unlikely that Carlyle circulated the manuscript among other publishers with the fictional Editor stating that the book seemed suitable only for *Fraser's* and that finally an agreement had been formed with Oliver Yorke, the fictional editor of *Fraser's* (*Sartor*, pp. 11–12). These particular remarks, the Oliver Yorke footnote on p. 13, and the final paragraph of the book, including a reference to Oliver Yorke and the attitude of British readers "during these current months" (pp. 297–98), were added either just before or, more likely, just after he reached an agreement with *Fraser's*. These changes are slight, and there seems little reason to suspect that there were greater ones.

May. Fraser reported to Carlyle that the serialized *Sartor* "meets with the most unqualified disapproval" (*Letters*, 2:128).

Sartor was not well adapted for serial publication. As Richard Garnett said, periodical publication placed *Sartor* at a disadvantage, allowing intervening distractions to obscure Carlyle's drift.[26] The structure of *Sartor* simply does not lend itself to the kinds of dramatic pauses novelists like Dickens soon learned to use so effectively. In *Fraser's*, "The Everlasting No" was separated from the "Centre of Indifference" and "The Everlasting Yea" by a month and by articles on such subjects as "National Economy," "Church and State in America," "Mare's Nests Found by the Materialists, the Owenites, and the Craniologists," and "Men and Manners: A Series of Satires: By Pierce Pungent" (*Fraser's*, 9 [1834], 301–455). And an installment of *Sartor* that began, "Though, after this 'Baphometic Fire-Baptism' of his, our Wanderer signifies that his Unrest was but increased," could only be considered unfortunate (*Fraser's*, 9 [1834], 443).[27] The context in which such language can operate effectively must be built up carefully. The book also suffered from not being read as a whole. Emerson, who told Carlyle not to be disappointed by its unpopularity in periodical form ("for if a memoir from Laplace had been thrown into that muckheap of Frasers Magazine, who would be the wiser?"), ate his "words of objection" to the first four installments when he had read the whole

[26] *Life of Thomas Carlyle*, Great Writers Series (London: Walter Scott, 1887), p. 68.
[27] Cf. "Critic of the Sun," *Sartor*, p. 320.

work.[28] Carlyle himself felt the work also suffered in periodical form from the audience it obtained. His extreme statement on the matter came in response to Sterling's rather presumptuous criticisms.[29] Carlyle defended his right to give up "mere dictionary Style" with "the whole structure of our Johnsonian English breaking up from its foundations," yet conceded several points as he went. But when Sterling attacked his ideas, it was too much for Carlyle. To Sterling's question of why the Clothes Philosophy has evoked no response, he replies, "It issued thro' one of the main *cloacas* of Periodical Literature, where no leading mind, I fancy, looks, if he can help it" (*Letters to Mill*, p. 192).

Carlyle was vindicated in his efforts to create a "book," something independent of the periodicals and not adapted to magazine publication, by *Sartor's* acceptance as a book; but its association with *Fraser's* and what he felt to be the restrictive conditions under which *Sartor* was made lingered in his critical attitude toward

[28] *The Correspondence of Emerson and Carlyle*, ed. Joseph Slater (New York: Columbia Univ. Press, 1964), pp. 107, 98. Emerson's description of *Fraser's* may have been influenced by what he knew to be Carlyle's own judgment of the magazine. See *English Traits*, ed. Howard Mumford Jones (Cambridge, Mass.: Belknap Press of Harvard Univ. Press, 1966), p. 9.

[29] Carlyle and Sterling were new acquaintances. See David Alec Wilson, *Carlyle to "The French Revolution" (1826–1837)*, Vol. II of *Life of Thomas Carlyle*, 6 vols. (London: Kegan Paul, 1923–34), p. 372, cited hereafter as D. A. Wilson, 2, and see *Letters*, 2:327–28. When Sterling sent his letter to him, Carlyle told John that Sterling had sent "a vituperative expostulary criticism on *Teufelsdröckh* of thirteen pages" (*Letters*, 2:332). Harrold reprints Sterling's letter and part of Carlyle's (*Sartor*, pp. 305–18), though not the remark quoted in the text just below.

the book. It was the best he could do in these times, he
felt. A late emendation in the book reflects his desire to
locate *Sartor* in a particular time. The *Fraser's* text gives
the full title of *"Die Kleider, ihr Werden und Wirken*
(Clothes, their Origin and Influence): *von Diog. Teufelsdröckh, J. U. D. etc. Stillschweigen und Cognie. Weissnichtwo, 1833" (Fraser's,* 8:582).[30] Modern editions give
the publication date of *Die Kleider* as 1831 (*Sartor*, p. 8),
after the London edition of *Sartor* (Saunders and Otley)
of 1838.[31] Carlyle, or perhaps his publisher, James Fraser,
probably used the 1833 date for *Fraser's* to make *Die
Kleider* contemporary. Carlyle alone, however, could
have dated the work back to the precise time in which it
was written. He did so because he felt the work, as far as
he as author was concerned, belonged to the time and
conditions of 1831.[32] He always recognized *Sartor* as an
adaptation to the times, and he maintained that posture
in spite of always increasing evidence that the book was
both popular and effective, indeed more popular and effective than some of his less compromising works. Carlyle's standards for himself were incredibly high, and his
willingness to modify his speech to make it more accept-

[30] See Tennyson, *Sartor Called Resartus*, pp. 204–05, on the title
of *Sartor*.

[31] The copy of this edition that I examined is in the Carlyle collection in the Hawthorne-Longfellow Library at Bowdoin College.
Carlyle read proof on this edition. See Dyer, p. 223; *New Letters
of Thomas Carlyle*, ed. Alexander Carlyle (London: John Lane,
1904), I, 128–29; *Letters to Alexander*, p. 441.

[32] See also the note Carlyle added to the 1869 Library Edition
of *Sartor* (Dyer, p. 226), where he says, "This questionable little
book was undoubtedly written among the mountain solitudes, in
1831" (*Sartor*, p. 319).

able and thereby more convincing was by contrast not very great. "Think of poor *me* and poor *Fraser's Magazine!*" he wrote Mill on 28 October 1833, the month before *Sartor* began in *Fraser's*. "Yet such is my *best* speaking mechanism at this moment; for aught I know, it is my only one" (*Letters to Mill*, p. 80).

Instead of suffering, as Carlyle thought, a kind of contamination from its association with *Fraser's* and the necessities imposed on Carlyle by circumstances, the work profited by both. Without its maker's complete approval, "the old Puttock Teufelsdröckh"[33] did quite well in the world. Carlyle made a form that was so effective by submitting his persuasive intention to conditions imposed on him and using them to advantage. He created a voice to speak effectively to a broad audience whose precise state of mind he in his isolation could not be certain of. He made his arguments broad and full, answering the kind of opposition he felt was present. He accommodated his audience even more fully by making his conditions a part of his persuasive form. Through the Editor he points to the plainness of Teufelsdröckh's speech and his apparent "rusticity and academic seclusion" (p. 29). The Editor even remarks that in spite of his *Sartor*'s suitability to *Fraser's*, the magazine is "in any case, understood to be, of late years, a vehicle full to overflowing, and inexorably shut" (p. 11). When he considers his biographical task, the Editor consoles himself for his efforts by asking, "And what work nobler than transplanting foreign Thought into the barren domestic soil; except indeed

[33] Carlyle's phrase, from a letter to his brother Alexander of 24 October 1834, *Letters*, 2:227.

planting Thought of your own, which the fewest are privileged to do?" (p. 80). The Editor's remarks, like Carlyle's similar remarks during the writing of *Sartor*, have a certain poignancy. Poor Carlyle, we begin to feel, who has to offer his own thought at first through a magazine and through a fictional contrivance that appears to be "transplanting foreign Thought." But such feelings disappear immediately when we recognize anew the astonishing power Carlyle was able to give his speech, without "privilege." In its context, the Editor's remark takes on a certain irony, because we know Carlyle is "planting Thought" of his own from the start, that he is making "privilege" where there appears to be none. Regardless of Carlyle's feelings about them, the circumstances that directed his genius into an original, powerful, and effective mode of persuasive essay were fortunate circumstances. They helped him achieve in *Sartor* a power he might not otherwise have attained.

His explanation of his unusual rhetoric to Emerson corroborates this view of *Sartor*. Feeling some disparity in *Sartor* between the vehicle and the ideas, Emerson asked Carlyle about the theory of his rhetoric and received this reply:

With regard to style and so forth, what you call your "saucy" objections are not only most intelligible to me, but welcome and instructive. You say well that I take up that attitude because I have no known public, am *alone* under the Heavens, speaking into friendly or unfriendly space; add only that I will not defend such attitude, that I call it questionable, tentative, and only the best that I in these mad times could conveniently hit upon. For you are to know, my view is that now at last we have lived to see all manner of Poetics and Rhetorics and Sermonics, and one may say generally all manner of *Pulpits* for addressing mankind from, as good as broken and abolished: alas, yes; if you have any earnest meaning, which demands to be not only listened to but *believed* and *done*, you cannot (at least I cannot) utter it *there*, but the sound sticks in my throat, as when a Solemnity were *felt* to have become a Mummery; and so one leaves the pasteboard coulisses, and three unities, and Blairs lectures, quite behind; and feels only that there is *nothing sacred*, then, but the *Speech of Man* to believing Men!

[*The Correspondence of Emerson and Carlyle,* pp. 103–04]

Carlyle saw *Sartor* as a way of speaking forth to move men to belief and action, a way of propagating his "earnest meaning, which demands to be not only listened to but *believed* and *done*."

Carlyle made a few changes in the apparatus of *Sartor* in its book form, changes designed to control further the reader's sense of what the text before him is and what is important in it. In the 1838 edition he added the "Testimonies of Authors" (Dyer, p. 223), and in the 1869 Library Edition he added a summary, broken up into the headnotes in Harrold's edition, and an index (Dyer, pp. 225–26).[34] In the "Testimonies of Authors" Carlyle includes the remarks of whoever read *Sartor* for Murray and Murray's own remarks to Carlyle about the book, under the title, "Highest Class, Bookseller's Taster."[35]

[34] He also added a note, referred to above, about the composition of *Sartor,* which Harrold prints under "Testimonies of Authors" (*Sartor,* p. 319).

[35] Carlyle thought Lockhart had been Murray's taster. See Sir Charles Gavan Duffy, *Conversations with Carlyle* (London: S. Low, Marston and Co., 1892), p. 20.

He then includes part of a review from the *Sun News-paper* attacking the book's style and unintelligibility. These reproaches are balanced and overcome by a long excerpt by a North American reviewer and a portion of Emerson's introduction to the American edition of *Sartor*. The North American reviewer considers quite carefully the evidence against the work's having any German origin and concludes it to be "in reality a treatise upon the great science of Things in General." He objects a bit soberly to its being passed off as "an Essay on Dress," but only because "the real subject of the work is to us more attractive than the ostensible one" (*Sartor*, p. 323). Emerson will not attempt to justify "the gay costume" or the "quaint and burlesque style," but assures prospective readers "that the foreign dress and aspect of the Work are quite superficial, and cover a genuine Saxon heart" and that "the manifest design of the work . . . is, a Criticism upon the Spirit of the Age—we had almost said, of the hour—in which we live" (*Sartor*, pp. 324–25). The two latter testimonies not only reflect badly on the superficiality of the English critics' remarks—and reflect well, of course, on *Sartor*—but they are also a guard against misunderstanding the book, especially since they appeared originally ahead of the text (Dyer, p. 223).

Carlyle's summary of *Sartor* is helpful to the reader, and it too calls attention to the essential ideas of the work, not, incidentally, to character development and especially not to conflict between the Editor and Teufelsdröckh. The index, too, points to ideas and away from plot and characters. One item in the index is particularly interesting. Under "*Sartor Resartus*," Carlyle lists "its purpose."[36] The reference is to the opening of Chapter IX of Book Third, "Circumspective," where the Editor asks if the Philosophy of Clothes is "opening around" British readers at last. The Editor continues: "Long and adventurous has the journey been: from those outmost vulgar, palpable Woollen Hulls of Man; through his wondrous Flesh-Garment, and his wondrous Social Garnitures; inwards to the Garments of his very Soul's Soul, to Time and Space themselves! And now does the spiritual, eternal Essence of Man, and of Mankind, bared of such wrappages, begin in any measure to reveal itself? Can many readers discern, as through a glass darkly, in wavering outlines, some primeval rudiments of Man's Being, what is changeable divided from what is unchangeable?" (Library Edition, p. 258).[37] If we couple this passage with a line from Carlyle's summary of "Circumspective," we have a clear idea of what Carlyle felt his book was intended to accomplish: "The true use of the *Sartor Resartus*, to exhibit the Wonder of daily life and common things; and to show that all Forms are but Clothes, and temporary" (Library Edition, p. 303). We need not always trust an author's view of his work, but these bits

---

[36] *Sartor Resartus: The Life and Opinions of Herr Teufelsdröckh: in Three Books*, Vol. I of *Collected Works*, Library Edition (London: Chapman and Hall, 1870), p. 307. Cited in the text as Library Edition. I have used this index because Harrold's incorporates Carlyle's in a larger one and modifies it somewhat.

[37] It may be argued that the Editor is talking about the effect of his own *Sartor Resartus*, not of Carlyle's. Since the meaninglessness of this distinction may not yet be clear, it should be noted that in the index and in the summary, quoted just below, Carlyle does not choose to indicate any distinction. He says "the *Sartor Resartus*," not "the Editor's *Sartor Resartus*."

of evidence become a part of the text and necessarily control our sense of what *Sartor* is.

In reading *Sartor* we may well feel the directness Carlyle thought his speech had, but explaining the basis of that feeling is difficult. In his remarks about and descriptions of the book, Carlyle pays remarkably little attention to the fact that his work contains sustained fictions. He calls the work *Teufelsdreck*, refers to the Editor, and calls it feebly "a kind of Didactic Novel," and he insists on the directness with which it persuades men of his creed. In the letter to Emerson quoted above, he admits his rhetoric is "questionable, tentative, and only the best that I in these mad times could conveniently hit upon." But he does not explain his fictions and how they contribute to his intention. In a letter to John Stuart Mill, however, he described certain kinds of fictions that allow a man to speak both tactfully and effectively. He told Mill of his discovery in January 1834, while *Sartor* was being published in *Fraser's Magazine*:

I approve greatly your purpose to discard Cant and Falsehood of all kinds: yet there is a kind of Fiction which is not Falsehood, and has more effect in addressing men than many a Radical is aware of. This has struck me much of late years in considering *Blackwood* and *Fraser*; both these are furnished as it were with a kind of theatrical costume, with orchestra and stage-lights, and thereby alone have a wonderful advantage; perhaps almost their only advantage. For nothing was ever truer than this, *Ubi homines sunt modi sunt*; a maxim which grows with me in significance the longer I meditate it; modifying innumerable things in my Philosophy.

[*Letters to Mill*, p. 93]

To most readers, fictions appear to be a barrier to direct speech, a kind of disguise. This response to fictions is deep seated. "If a man wishes to speak, let him speak to us in his own voice," we think instinctively. But Carlyle saw them as a way of speaking the truth effectively. My purpose is to explain how, as Carlyle suggests, *Sartor*'s fictional mode is a particularly powerful mode of speaking to the reader to effect his persuasive intention, perhaps the most powerful available to Carlyle.

3: The Editor and the Controlling Voice in *Sartor*

The device of making a book by pretending to edit the papers of another person may appear to be rather a stale one, and has certainly been of late pressed quite unconscionably into the service. But in the present instance it was absolutely essential to the management of the author's plan, and has been so ingeniously availed of as quite to reconcile us to it.

N. L. FROTHINGHAM ON *Sartor Resartus* [1]

ONE of the ways in which Carlyle speaks to us is through the fictional Editor. While at times the Editor is given the appearance of being a particular character in the narrative, he is in fact a flexible rhetorical device whose attitudes at any given moment are determined by Carlyle's persuasive purpose. As we read, we are interested in the Editor's comments on Teufelsdröckh's ideas as they aid our own understanding of and fix our attitude toward the Clothes Philosophy. We are not interested in the Editor's comments as they reveal his character or as they reveal a progression in the Editor's relationship to Teufelsdröckh or to the materials the Editor works with. Our interest is in coming to know the Clothes Philosophy, not the fate of the Editor. Any incipient interest in his fate or charac-

[1] "Sartor Resartus," *Christian Examiner*, 21 (1836), 77.

ter is carefully controlled in order to maintain our interest in the Clothes Philosophy and is never allowed to
usurp interest from that set of ideas.[2]

Those who call *Sartor* a novel or narrative representation see the Editor as a discrete character who is consistently represented or who should be consistently represented. The Editor is obviously crucial to any view of the
book as a novel. He is present throughout the book, and
his relationship with Teufelsdröckh appears to be a central one among those that ought to absorb our interest.
The consequences of applying to *Sartor* the standards of
novelistic criticism, as they are put forth by those who
call the book a novel and by other formal critics, are se-
vere. Measured against great novels by standards of plot,
characterization, consistency, action, *Sartor* must be
placed low on the scale. The story of an Editor struggling
to comprehend and to shape a mass of documents by a
mysterious German philosopher looks insubstantial and
uninteresting next to *Emma, Great Expectations*, or *Middlemarch*, and even against lesser nineteenth-century

[2] Sheldon Sacks says that "some forms of apologues—e.g.,
Jonathan Wild and *Candide*—make more use than *Rasselas* does
of the qualities which impart vividness to characters, but impose
other kinds of restrictions to suppress the expectations appropriate
only in actions. The general postulation that the job of the writer
of [an] apologue is to maximize our interest in the agents to the
greatest degree possible short of obscuring the relation of any epi-
sode to its controlling theme is applicable to all forms of apologue"
(Sacks, p. 60n). A similar rule applies in *Sartor*. Carlyle will maximize our interest in a character or his fate when it is to his rhetorical advantage to do so, always limiting the kinds of expectations appropriate to actions or novels. Since Carlyle is writing a
form of argument and not a novel, vividness in characterization is
present more frequently as vividness in speech than as vividness
in description or in activity.

novels. In fact, such a subject for a novel seems impossible. Would readers of Scott and Edgeworth settle for a dry Editor wrestling with German transcendentalism? Furthermore, if such a plot could have any psychological power or human interest, it is not given such power or interest in *Sartor.* Finally, the standards of novelistic criticism are not a satisfactory means of measuring the power and value of the book.

Sartor simply does not work as a novel works, and the fictional device of the Editor, far from being another defect in a bad novel, is one of the strengths of this persuasive work. If we look closely at what the Editor says, we see that he is not carefully discriminated from Teufelsdröckh, that he is not developed consistently or interestingly, and that he is not involved in any absorbing, carefully articulated conflict at all. If we search for the conflict some claim to be the motivating conflict of the book, we find few grounds for saying that it exists at all. From the beginning the Editor is favorably disposed to Teufelsdröckh and to his book, *Die Kleider.* He has some difficulty understanding Teufelsdröckh's ideas, but very early in the book the Clothes Volume, "read and again read, was in several points becoming lucid and lucent" (p. 11). The Editor resolves to publish his own edition of *Die Kleider:* "For if new-got gold is said to burn the pockets till it be cast forth into circulation, much more may new truth." The Editor's faith in Teufelsdröckh is easily won and complete. He already sees the Clothes Philosophy as "new truth" to be published abroad. Surely Carlyle could create greater conflict, could arouse more complex expectations about this character, could work a more interesting plot. The Editor could be made indisposed to *Die Kleider* and won over to it in a complicated way. Expectations could be raised from the beginning, perhaps, that he might be overcome with melancholy and die of mad despair unless he could be saved by the enigmatic German treatise.

The only complexity Carlyle allows is the Editor's difficulty in understanding and arranging the *Sartor Resartus* which he is creating out of *Die Kleider* and the biographical materials Hofrath Heuschrecke has promised to supply. But the potential psychological conflicts that surround the Editor's struggles are stated in very special terms. In Chapter XI, Prospective, the Editor says that the Philosophy of Clothes is unfolding before the reader, though he may be puzzled about its meaning and its value: "Ever higher and dizzier are the heights he leads us to" (p. 71). The Editor quotes several passages from *Die Kleider* which state explicitly the essential notion that the real world is spiritual and is to be seen through emblems or "Clothes," and concludes, "Thus in this one pregnant subject of CLOTHES, rightly understood, is included all that men have thought, dreamed, done or been: the whole External Universe and what it holds is but Clothing, and the essence of all Science lies in the PHILOSOPHY OF CLOTHES." At this point the Editor expresses frustration:

Towards these dim infinitely-expanded regions, close-bordering on the impalpable Inane, it is not without apprehension, and perpetual difficulties, that the Editor sees himself journeying and struggling. Till lately a cheerful daystar of hope hung before him, in the expected Aid of Hofrath Heuschrecke; which daystar, however, melts now not into the red of morning, but into a vague, gray half-light, uncertain whether dawn of day or dusk of utter darkness. For the last week, these so-called Biographical Documents are in his hand. By the kindness of a Scottish Hamburg Merchant . . . the bulky Weissnichtwo Packet, with all its Customhouse seals, foreign hieroglyphs, and miscellaneous tokens of Travel, arrived here in perfect safety, and free of cost. The reader shall now fancy with what hot haste it was broken up, with what breathless expectation glanced over; and, alas, with what unquiet disappointment it has, since then, been often thrown down, and again taken up.

[pp. 74–75]

This paragraph might be taken to be part of the Editor's intellectual and spiritual development or to be a phase of his personal relationship to Teufelsdröckh and his ideas. Yet we are told very little specifically about his state of mind, about the spiritual consequences of his not coming to understand the Clothes Philosophy. If the Editor is our hero, we want to know more about his inner tensions, his anxieties, the other possibilities open to him. We hardly want to be told to "fancy" for ourselves what he feels. The passage serves a purpose different from the revelation of a character in a particular situation, the advancement of a plot or narrative.

We are directed to "fancy" for ourselves because the Editor's situation here approximates or should approximate our own. At the very least it suggests to the reader a way of feeling about what he has been reading and about the shortcomings of the promised biography. The "daystar" that has been put before him "melts now, not into the red of morning, but into a vague, gray half-light, uncertain whether dawn or dusk or utter darkness." The terms in which the Editor expresses his search for understanding are exactly those of the Clothes Philosophy. He is to see into the spiritual world, now one of vague darkness, by means of an emblem, the biography that Heuschrecke promised. Thus, through the fiction of the Editor, the reader is conditioned to think about the process by which he is learning in terms of the world view being presented to him. That the Editor is represented as already thinking in these terms minimizes the effects of anything like a plot. The reader is not apart from the Editor, judging his actions, caring about what will happen to him. The reader is made to care more about what will happen to himself. Those who wish to see the book as a novel argue that the conflict is between the Editor and his materials. We might conceivably fear that the Editor may fail to present the Clothes Philosophy, to complete his *Sartor Resartus*; but we are made to fear most that we will not achieve complete understanding of the Clothes Philosophy. Our attention is constantly diverted from anything like narrative to the apprehension and growth of ideas in our own minds.

We are stimulated to action as well as to understanding. The Editor sees himself here, "journeying and struggling" toward understanding and later "struggling" to help English readers understand the Clothes Philosophy (p. 79). Again, Carlyle uses the Editor to enlist the reader in what is, in the world of the Clothes Philosophy, moral activity. Soon the Editor exhorts the reader to join him in making something intelligible out of the biographical fragments Heuschrecke has sent him: "Wild as it looks, this Philosophy of Clothes, can we ever reach its real meaning, promises to reveal new-coming Eras, the first dim rudiments and already-budding germs of a nobler Era, in Universal History. Is not such a prize worth some striving? Forward with us, courageous reader; be it to-

wards failure, or towards success! The latter thou sharest
with us; the former also is not all our own" (p. 80). The
Editor suggests the possibility of failure, but not the failure of the ideal, the Clothes Philosophy, rather the failure of the Editor and the reader to attain that ideal. Thus,
again, the Editor is used to encourage intellectual or spiritual striving, the doctrine of work applied to the spirit,
and to stimulate the reader to similar activity.[3] He suggests further the social responsibility, emphasized in
Book Third, of striving to spread the Clothes Philosophy.
What the Editor claims about *Die Kleider* Carlyle hopes
will be true about *Sartor*: "We [the Editor] admitted that
the Book had in a high degree excited us to self-activity,
which is the best effect of any book; that it had even
operated changes in our way of thought; nay, that it
promised to prove, as it were, the opening of a new mine-
shaft, wherein the whole world of Speculation might
henceforth dig to unknown depths" (p. 28). This remark
about *Die Kleider* is interesting because it opens up a
possibility for us, because it helps us define an attitude
toward the material the Editor is presenting, not because
it helps us to understand the Editor's character. In fact,
Carlyle takes some pains to keep us from becoming interested in the Editor as a character about whose fate we
might care, takes pains to focus our attention on the argument, not the person.

For example, when all the conditions for publishing

---

[3] In "State of German Literature," when explaining how a
writer with an "invisible and immaterial" object must win a reader, Carlyle says that "the reader must faithfully and toilsomely
cooperate with him, if any fruit is to come of their mutual endeavour" (*Works*, 26:72).

the Editor's *Sartor Resartus* are settled, when an agreement has been reached with *Fraser's* and documents seem forthcoming from Heuschrecke, the Editor tries to remove himself from the reader's interest in favor of his materials:

Of our fitness for the Enterprise, to which we have such title and vocation, it were perhaps uninteresting to say more. Let the British reader study and enjoy, in simplicity of heart, what is here presented him, and with whatever metaphysical acumen and talent for meditation he is possessed of. Let him strive to keep a free, open sense; cleared from the mists of prejudice, above all from the paralysis of cant; and directed rather to the Book itself than to the Editor of the Book. Who or what such Editor may be, must remain conjectural, and even insignificant:[1] it is a voice publishing tidings of the Philosophy of Clothes; undoubtedly a Spirit addressing Spirits: whoso hath ears, let him hear.

[1] With us even he still communicates in some sort of mask, or muffler; and, we have reason to think, under a feigned name!—O. Y.

[pp. 12–13]

The reader's attention is directed to the materials, and he is instructed to take a certain attitude toward them. Furthermore, Carlyle sacrifices much of his attempt to make the reader believe that the Editor's capacity is "historical and critical" (p. 14). The Editor sounds rather like a transcendentalist, though Carlyle's mocking footnote forces us to take the Editor less seriously than he begins to take himself, or at least to take him in a different way. In a narrative such toying would be destructive. Here Carlyle constantly prevents us from taking his fictions seriously, while at the same time he reinforces our sense that there is "a voice publishing tidings of the Philosophy of Clothes" speaking to us through the fictions, a voice less exalted perhaps than "a Spirit addressing Spirits" but firmer and finer than a comical figure "in some sort of mask, or muffler," who may even use a "feigned name."

It may be argued that I am oversimplifying the texture of *Sartor* if I suggest that there is one voice speaking to us about the Clothes Philosophy.[4] This brings us back to the question of conflict or disagreement between the Editor and Teufelsdröckh or Teufelsdröckh's written word. Yet in the Editor's relationship to Teufelsdröckh, the Editor's agreement and understanding appear to vary, but not according to any pattern that is intelligible in terms of the Editor's psychology or mental growth. Furthermore, what appears to be disagreement and conflict turns into qualified agreement or simply anticipation of certain kinds of objections leading to agreement. What determines the degree of the Editor's understanding or agreement is the particular light in which Carlyle wishes to place the material he is presenting at a given moment.

---

[4] George Levine, for example, says that "two people, not one, announce the doctrine of *Sartor*" and "the literal surface of that book is never whole-hearted and unambiguous" ("*Sartor Resartus* and the Balance of Fiction," p. 55). Levine defines some of the rhetorical functions of the Editor and then argues that the Editor represents Carlyle "sitting in dispassionate judgment on himself" (p. 57). Carlisle Moore in "Thomas Carlyle and Fiction, 1822–1834" argues in a similar vein. But, contrary to their arguments, Carlyle is no skeptic and brooks no real disagreement in *Sartor*. It would be easy to show, for example, that the Editor serves the functions of both the foolish reviewer and the serious reviewer, as Carlyle defines them in "Novalis," *Works*, 27:5–8. To do so would show further that Carlyle did not regard the Editor as a consistent character, capable of real, systematic disagreement.

The Editor's attitudes are determined by rhetorical considerations originating in Carlyle's persuasive purpose.[5]

At the beginning of Book First, Chapter IX, "Adamitism," the Editor appears to disagree with the Professor. Teufelsdröckh has just said that "there is something great in the moment when a man first strips himself of adventitious wrappages; and sees indeed that he is naked, and, as Swift has it 'a forked straddling animal with bandy legs'; yet also a Spirit, and unutterable Mystery of Mysteries" (p. 57). The Editor begins "Adamitism": "Let no courteous reader take offence at the opinions broached in the conclusion of the last Chapter. The Editor himself, on first glancing over that singular passage, was inclined to exclaim: What, have we got not only a Sansculottist, but an enemy to Clothes in the abstract? A new Adamite, in this century, which flatters itself that it is the Nineteenth, and destructive both to Superstition and Enthusiasm?" (pp. 57–58). These may be questions that rise in our heads and that we wish to have answered. Perhaps not, however; and if not, our pleasure in perceiving what Carlyle is doing will be increased. The Editor's innocent tone is rendered suspect immediately. He addresses Teufelsdröckh to chastise him for not remembering what importance clothes have, but the change in his tone betrays him. He addresses the "courteous reader" in a distinctly civilized, conservative,

[5] In *Carlyle and the Idea of the Modern*, Albert J. LaValley argues that the Editor participates in a kind of dialectic that is itself the writing of *Sartor*. He agrees that the Editor is a flexible device, not governed by the dynamics of characterization, but he feels that the Editor is governed by a spontaneous process of thought rather than by the demands of rhetoric or argument. See LaValley, pp. 89–103.

and somewhat naive tone. He addresses Teufelsdröckh, however, in the Professor's own tongue: "Consider, thou foolish Teufelsdröckh, what benefits unspeakable all ages and sexes derive from Clothes. For example, when thou thyself, a watery, pulpy, slobbery freshman and new-comer in this Planet, sattest muling and puking in thy nurse's arms; sucking thy coral, and looking forth into the world in the blankest manner, what hadst thou been without thy blankets, and bibs, and other nameless hulls? A terror to thyself and mankind!" (p. 58). The Editor rages on, and the mind begins to suspect, if it has not all along, his independence from Teufelsdröckh, his integrity as a character. He seems in conflict with Teufelsdröckh, but he slips so easily into the Professor's tone and style. In addition, his disagreement with Teufelsdröckh is tentative, based on the possibility that Teufelsdröckh has forgotten the benefits of clothes.

At the end of this tentative but forceful attack on Teufelsdröckh, the Editor has the reader join the fray: "Or, cries the courteous reader, has your Teufelsdröckh forgotten what he said lately about 'Aboriginal Savages,' and their 'condition miserable indeed'? Would he have all this unsaid; and us betake ourselves again to the 'matted cloak,' and go sheeted in a 'thick natural fell'?" (p. 59). The "courteous reader" may indeed wish to raise this second objection to Teufelsdröckh's remark. But if he does, he gets pummeled for his troubles:

Nowise, courteous reader! The Professor knows full well what he is saying; and both thou and we, in our haste, do him wrong. If Clothes, in these times "so tailorise and demoralise us," have they no redeeming value; can they not be altered to serve better; must they of necessity be thrown to the dogs? The truth is, Teufelsdröckh, though a Sansculottist, is no Adamite; and much perhaps as he might wish to go forth before this degenerate age as "a Sign," would nowise wish to do it, as those old Adamites did, in a state of Nakedness. The utility of Clothes is altogether apparent to him: nay perhaps he has an insight into their more recondite, and almost mystic qualities, what we might call the omnipotent virtue of Clothes, such as was never before vouchsafed to any man.

[p. 60]

What appeared to be conflict is turned to affirmation. Two objections, that Teufelsdröckh did not know the importance of clothes and that he had contradicted himself by advocating Adamitism, are raised and accounted for. The Editor's voice, shifting tone and style easily, and integrated carefully with what Teufelsdröckh has said, has furthered the argument that clothes must be scrutinized for their root value. Even the significance the Editor gives to "Clothes" is consistent with Teufelsdröckh's sense. The term "Sansculottist," with its intrinsic association of clothing with a political and even revolutionary stance, and the term "Adamitism," denoted as "Superstition" and "Enthusiasm," suggest that the Editor is talking in metaphors. When the Editor comes to suggest that clothes can be "altered to serve better," we know he is talking about social and political change. When he then says in the next sentence that "Teufelsdröckh, though a Sansculottist, is no Adamite," we have no difficulty following his meaning. Our apprehension of what is said here is geared to a complex and suggestive set of metaphors that operate independent of apparent distinctions between characters. Even the "courteous reader" asks the right questions, questions operating in the same context of meaning.

Another example will help to show further how fully coordinated the voices of the Editor and the German Professor are. Carlyle uses the Editor to reinforce some ideas and to suggest attitudes toward others. He is made to approve of Teufelsdröckh's definition of man as a "tool-using animal" (p. 41) and shortly thereafter warns that what Teufelsdröckh says about aprons is "one of the most unsatisfactory Sections in the whole Volume" (p. 43). Thus he appears to be impartial. But the Editor's tone and character cannot be simplified. What is going on in the instances just mentioned is very complicated. In the first, the Editor interrupts Teufelsdröckh's rather high-flown paragraph on man as a tool user. After approving of Teufelsdröckh's definition, he comments on a few other definitions, which he finds less plausible. He says, for example, "Still less do we make of that other French Definition of the cooking Animal; which, indeed, for rigorous scientific purposes, is as good as useless. Can a Tartar be said to cook when he only readies his steak by riding on it?" (pp. 41–42). He concludes, "But, on the other hand, show us the human being, of any period or climate, without his Tools: those very Caledonians, as we saw, had their Flint-ball, and Thong to it, such as no brute has or can have." Then Teufelsdröckh returns with a rather serious paragraph about man's present use of tools and thus of power:

"Man is a Tool-using Animal," concludes Teufelsdröckh in his abrupt way; "of which truth Clothes are but one example: and surely if we consider the interval between the first wooden Dibble fashioned by man, and those Liverpool Steam-carriages, or the British House of Commons, we shall note what progress he has made. He digs up certain black stones from the bosom of the earth, and says to them, *Transport me and this luggage at the rate of five-and-thirty miles an hour*; and they do it: he collects, apparently by lot, six-hundred and fifty-eight miscellaneous individuals, and says to them, *Make this nation toil for us, bleed for us, hunger and sorrow and sin for us*; and they do it."

[p. 42]

Arbitrary power that functions like the new railroad is a serious matter, especially in contrast with the Editor's fooling about cookery. The Editor does not tell the reader the matter at hand has become serious, as he might else-where, but his interruption has prepared the way for Teufelsdröckh's gloomy words. First of all, the Editor has effected a radical shift in tone. Teufelsdröckh had risen to great heights in praise of man's use of tools: "With these the granite mountain melts into light dust before him; he kneads glowing iron, as if it were soft paste; seas are his smooth highway, winds and fire his unwearying steeds" (p. 41). The Editor's breaking in, disparaging this "stream of Oratory" and playing with other definitions in a mockery of "rigorous scientific purposes," has al-lowed the reader to reassess Teufelsdröckh's definition of man without the pressure of the prophet's high rhet-oric. In fact, the Editor pleads for his acceptance of that definition as the least foolish of many foolish ones. Fur-thermore, the Editor effects a necessary transition to Teu-felsdröckh's closing paragraph about man as a tool-using animal. By reminding us of rude Caledonians, mentioned several pages before by Teufelsdröckh (p. 39), with their "Flint-ball and Thong," the Editor introduces a vision of

primitive man which makes more effective Teufelsdröckh's vision of modern man presented in the next
paragraph. The Editor also permits Carlyle one of his
favorite devices, juxtaposing a comic view on a serious
one in order to force assessment of both. Thus Carlyle
uses the two voices to work subtle, or sometimes not
subtle, integrated changes in tone and subject.

Carlyle's procedure here is, of course, not logical. Teufelsdröckh presents a view of man as a supremely powerful being, wielding the elements as his tools. Then he
offers a diminished view of man, submitting himself arbitrarily to "six hundred and fifty-eight miscellaneous
individuals." Man is not brought down from the heights
of power by careful argument, but by a transition in tone
and direction worked by the intervention of the Editor.
As we read such passages, we are not interested continuously in the Editor's character and his relationship to
Teufelsdröckh or his materials. Here we are made to feel
that we are foolish to give up arbitrarily our tremendous
natural power. We become prepared to act on our new,
growing belief in the Clothes Philosophy, to throw off
submissiveness. In fact, as the reader becomes more familiar with the Clothes Philosophy, he becomes less and
less aware of the division of what he reads into two
voices. He responds almost as he would if there were one
voice speaking to him, and he becomes aware of direct
conflict between the two or any other facet of the distinction between the two characters only when Carlyle forces
him to, in order to confirm some aspect of the Clothes
Philosophy. This effect gradually increases the reader's
sense of independence and self-confidence. Finding himself able to interpret any conflict presented and having

his interpretations reinforced by the one voice, the reader finds strength in his new belief.[6]

The frequent merging of the voices of the apparent narrative into one in the reader's mind is produced by what might be called the "implied orator."[7] The reader perceives intuitively what I have tried to make explicit, that all elements of *Sartor* work to make him believe in the Clothes Philosophy. This cumulative sense of what Carlyle is about, aided by implicit signals, helps the reader to interpret what any given voice says to him. This effect may appear to be similar to that of the "implied author" of a novel, but it is actually quite different. In a novel we are aware, in varying degrees, of a mind arranging the plot and evaluating the characters, points of view, and activities that make up the plot. In *Sartor* we are aware of one mind sorting and arranging and evaluating ideas, characters, experiences in relation to the Clothes Philosophy, and of one mind carrying on an argument. We know that everything presented is there because of its relevance to the Clothes Philosophy and is evaluated according to the Clothes Philosophy. The constant and conspicuous manipulation of the materials to favor the Clothes Philosophy makes us sense the presence of that one "voice publishing tidings." What is determined by the implied orator is our attitude toward a set of ideas in our own minds, our response to words addressed directly to us, not, as in a novel, our attitude to-

[6] This sense of confidence was pointed out to me by Professor James L. Battersby.

[7] This term is derived from Wayne Booth's discussion of the "implied author" of novels in *The Rhetoric of Fiction*, pp. 70–77. G. B. Tennyson notes that the attitude of an "implied author" plays over *Sartor* (*Sartor Called Resartus*, p. 183n).

ward characters in an action about whose fates we are
made to care. The reader's sense of the "implied orator"
is more constant and more immediate than is his sense of
the "implied author" in most novels.

It is the implied orator that allows the reader to interpret occasional disagreement between the Editor and
Teufelsdröckh, and this interpretation always favors the
Clothes Philosophy. Another example may make this
clear. In the chapter on "Aprons" the Editor is made to
appear not fully to understand or appreciate Teufelsdröckh's fancies. He sees "sometimes even a tone of
levity, approaching to conventional satire" (p. 43). But
the material the Editor passes off as incomprehensible
"stuff" is quite radical material (p. 44). Teufelsdröckh
remarks that the "Overseer (*Episcopus*) of Souls" has
tucked in the corner of his apron, "as if his day's work
were done: what does he shadow forth thereby?" (p. 45,
n). The Editor does not take seriously Teufelsdröckh's
next statement that "the Journalists are now the true
Kings and Clergy." This idea, however, is one that Carlyle takes seriously and one that will be urged on the
reader more openly and without qualification later in the
book.[8] Carlyle often presents ideas tentatively at first.
Here the Editor's bland response, as well as Teufelsdröckh's playfulness, is a means of curbing the power of
these ideas temporarily, of forcing the reader to his own
assessment where he is dissatisfied with the Editor's, and
of controlling the reader who is unsympathetic to the

[8] Harrold's note (p. 45) attests to the seriousness with which
Carlyle takes this idea: "Cf. 'Quintus Fixlein' (*German Romance*,
II, 304–05); *On Heroes*, pp. 162–63; *Ess.*, II, 77."

Clothes Philosophy. Objection and criticism seem increasingly fruitless.

The reader's growing sense of the presence of the implied orator both guides him through difficulties and allows Carlyle to confirm ideas in indirect but effective ways. At the end of the passage we have been examining, Teufelsdröckh claims ironically to have searched the Weissnichtwo libraries for a history of the British newspaper press, titled *"Satan's Invisible World Displayed"* (p. 45). The Editor, for those readers without Harrold's always informative notes, supplies the necessary information: "Thus does the good Homer not only nod, but snore. Thus does Teufelsdröckh, wandering in regions where he had little business, confound the old authentic Presbyterian Witchfinder with a new, spurious, imaginary Historian of *Brittische Journalistik*; and so stumble on perhaps the most egregious blunder in Modern Literature!" (p. 46). Homer may nod, but the reader is forced, by the Editor's obvious misunderstanding of the joke, to admit that Teufelsdröckh is ever alert. Everything the reader has perceived about Teufelsdröckh and the Clothes Philosophy urges him to believe that Teufelsdröckh means to be critical of the British press. The implied orator guides the reader through.[9]

[9] Carlisle Moore in "Thomas Carlyle and Fiction, 1822–1834" makes similar remarks about Carlyle's ironic use of the Editor and Teufelsdröckh, but he feels Carlyle does this to preserve his hoax and gull the reader, on the assumption that if Carlyle wished merely to persuade, he would use "a simpler method of presenting his ideas" (p. 152). In this view *Sartor's* complex method, then, must result from his purely unphilosophical, irrational love of hoaxing. I have tried to suggest that the hoax or fictional elements

As the book progresses, Carlyle is careful to keep our attention on the argument the implied orator is making and not on the fictional characters. In a passage discussed above, he has the Editor call attention away from himself and to the materials and has him identify himself as a "voice publishing tidings of the Philosophy of Clothes." At the end of Book Third, Chapter I, "Incident in Modern History," Carlyle calls attention once again to the way the materials in the book are arranged and evaluated according to one persuasive purpose. As in the passage from "Adamitism" discussed above, the Editor chastises Teufelsdröckh for a deficiency in his argument. Teufelsdröckh has presented the story of George Fox who stitched himself a leather suit and went to live in the woods and to feed on wild berries. The Editor sees Teufelsdröckh's point and remarks on it: "Does Teufelsdröckh anticipate that, in this age of refinement, any considerable class of the community, by way of testifying against the 'Mammon-god,' and escaping from what he calls 'Vanity's Workhouse and Ragfair,' where doubtless some of them are toiled and whipped and hood-winked sufficiently,—will sheathe themselves in close-fitting cases of Leather? The idea is ridiculous in the extreme" (p. 212). We interpret this passage ironically; that is, our sense of what the implied orator is about leads us to see it not as a criticism of Teufelsdröckh or his ideas but as a criticism of those who will not act according to them, who will not clothe themselves properly.

---

of *Sartor* serve the persuasive purpose rather than thwart it. As John Sterling remarked in his review, "Carlyle's Works," the "jest" in *Sartor* is "pretence" and "the purport of the whole is serious" (*London and Westminster Review*, 33 [1839], 53).

In case we misinterpret the irony, in case we feel some genuine conflict between Teufelsdröckh and the Editor, Carlyle has the Editor call attention to the larger pattern of argument. After more questions about the possibility of the established classes giving up anything, the Editor remarks, "Or has the Professor his own deeper intention; and laughs in his sleeve at our strictures and glosses, which indeed are but a part thereof?" (p. 213). We are not likely to attribute godlike control of the Editor's speech to Teufelsdröckh, but instead we are forced to recognize the care the implied orator has used in integrating what his two fictions say. The Editor's "strictures and glosses" are part of a "deeper intention." If, on the other hand, we couple this remark with a few other hints given in the book, we might be inclined to attribute what the Editor says to Teufelsdröckh's manipulation. The Editor uses Teufelsdröckh's figurative language and Germanisms, and he comments on doing so (pp. 287, 293). Their similarity in this respect and their general agreement, the Editor's communicating with *Fraser's* "in some kind of mask, or muffler; and, we have reason to think, under a feigned name!" (p. 13n), and the Editor's guess at the end of the book that "Teufelsdröckh is actually in London!" (p. 297) might lead us to suspect that Teufelsdröckh and the Editor are the same man. There is no need to press this point. Carlyle himself does not, and it barely changes our perception of how *Sartor* is constructed. We feel the Editor and Teufelsdröckh as reflexes of the same mind without Carlyle's gentle joke that they may be the same man.[10] The remark simply confirms the referential

[10] Carlyle thought quite carefully about the effects he achieved with his fictions. In describing proposed apparatus for his "Dia-

quality of the book, confirms what the reader has known for a long time, not that Teufelsdröckh is identical with the author, but that the book speaks for a real man concerned with real English problems.

The effect of the implied orator is not a defect in the work.[11] *Sartor* works through fictions in which a single, true voice is implicit. Our whole sense of the unity of *Sartor* depends on our continuous grasp of the effect the implied orator has on us. If making characters act according to their discriminate personalities distracts the reader from the flow of argument, then consistency of characterization must be violated. Carlyle must keep our attention on the Clothes Philosophy, and one way in which he does this is by subordinating consistent representation of discriminate characters to the persuasive presentation of his ideas. It is necessary in *Sartor* to maintain minimal consistency, to keep the Editor and Teufelsdröckh distinguished and distinguishable. In some cases the two can be distinguished by the different styles Carlyle creates for them. Often, however, they both use the same

---

mond Necklace" to Mill in 1834, he said, "I will speak of it as being 'in rhyme in the *original*' (which it partly was), and so forth; and give it a kind of quizzical garniture, thro' which the true authorship may peer out clearly enough" (*Letters to Mill*, pp. 104–05).

[11] In "Relationship of Style and Device in *Sartor Resartus*," Daniel P. Deneau argues that Carlyle's failure to discriminate stylistically between the Editor and Teufelsdröckh is "a significant flaw" in the book (p. 201). He argues that there is "a single voice in *Sartor* which raises and lowers its tone" according to the "emotional force of the moment," but he sees this as a weakness because it interferes with proper representation of separate characters (p. 19). Masao Miyoshi, on the other hand, calls *Sartor* "a masterpiece of voice manipulation" in *The Divided Self: A Perspective on the Literature of the Victorians* (New York: New York Univ. Press, 1969), p. 138.

syntactical patterns, particularly the sentence full of qualifying phrases, typical of Carlyle's general usage.[12] Furthermore, Carlyle uses this same style in both fictional characters to say many of the same things, as we have seen.[13] In general the effort required to maintain consistency is minimal, often involving only the placement of quotation marks and phrases identifying the speaker.

The point to be made is that frequently and conspicuously what the Editor says embodies knowledge and an intention and implies a mind, all of which can only be understood to be that of the person behind Teufelsdröckh and the whole persuasive impulse of the book. The Editor remarks at the end of the book that he has taken on some of the characteristics of Teufelsdröckh's way of speaking. This occurrence might be taken as a sign of a full shift of the Editor's sympathy with Teufelsdröckh, a sign of the resolution of the plot of *Sartor*, the plot conceived as a conflict between the Editor and his materials. But the Editor's assumption of Teufels-

[12] Josephine Miles, *Style and Proportion: The Language of Prose and Poetry* (Boston: Little, Brown, 1967), p. 59. Miss Miles refers us to Grace J. Calder, *The Writing of Past and Present*.

[13] See G. B. Tennyson's remarks on style in *Sartor*. He implies that there is a uniform and didactic style in the book (*Sartor Called Resartus*, pp. 238–59). See also, of course, John Holloway's chapter "Carlyle" in *The Victorian Sage: Studies in Argument* (London: Macmillan, 1953), pp. 21–57; Frederick L. Burwick, "Stylistic Continuity and Change in the Prose of Thomas Carlyle," in *Statistics and Style* (Math. Ling. and Auto. Lang. Processing 6.), ed. Lubomír Dolezel and Richard W. Bailey (New York: Amer. Elsevier, 1969), 178–96; and Richard Ohmann, "A Linguistic Appraisal of Victorian Style," in *The Art of Victorian Prose*, ed. George Levine and William Madden (New York: Oxford Univ. Press, 1968), pp. 289–313.

dröckh's manner and the implied orator's, which is seldom very distant from Teufelsdröckh's, predates the end
of the book considerably.

The first sentence of *Sartor* renders impossible any
view of the Editor as naive and conservative or essentially different from Teufelsdröckh. *Sartor* begins,

Considering our present advanced state of culture, and how
the Torch of Science has now been brandished and borne
about, with more or less effect, for five thousand years and
upwards; how, in these times especially, not only the Torch
still burns, and perhaps more fiercely than ever, but innumerable Rush-lights, and Sulphur-matches, kindled thereat,
are also glancing in every direction, so that not the smallest
cranny or doghole in Nature or Art can remain unilluminated,
—it might strike the reflective mind with some surprise that
hitherto little or nothing of a fundamental character, whether
in the way of Philosophy or History, has been written on the
subject of Clothes.

[p. 3]

This sentence implies a unique and startling mind. It
pauses in the midst of a rather neutral periodic sentence
to present a picture of a mad world where Science rushes
into every corner. If we take the first participial phrase
and link it with the main clause, we have a rather straight-
forward and uninteresting introduction to a book on
clothes: "Considering our present advanced state of culture, it might strike the reflective mind with some surprise
that hitherto little or nothing of a fundamental character,
whether in the way of Philosophy or History, has been
written on the subject of Clothes." This sentence might
be written by a conservative British editor. But what goes
on among the qualifying phrases alters completely our

sense of what is said and what the writer of the full sentence is like. He sees science as a torch not simply "borne"
but "brandished" about, a menacing weapon. Today the
torch burns "perhaps more fiercely than ever" and is an
even greater threat. There is more than the big torch to
worry about. Its emissaries, "innumerable Rush-lights
and Sulphur-matches," like suspicious eyes are "glancing in every direction." They light everything indiscrimi-
nately even "the smallest cranny or doghole." The realm
in which they carry on their threatening and ill-directed
activities is a surprise, the sacred realm of "Nature and
Art." This vision of a world beset by science determines
our apprehension of who the Editor is and what he is
doing. Without it we would be prepared for another
treatise presented by a rather conventional, mild personality. With it we suspect the very validity of treatises,
of the kind of thing the book before us purports in some
respects to be. The opening sentence, moreover, associates *Sartor* with the conventions of *Fraser's Magazine*.
The mock historical perspective, characterizing the age
while diminishing it ironically, was a mode of beginning
essays in *Fraser's*.[14] It is a parody of and depends for its
ironic effects on the kind of serious opening sentence

[14] See, for example, "Remarkable Vision of Charles XI of Sweden," *Fraser's*, 1 (1830), 120; "The Dominie's Legacy," 1 (1830),
318; "On Medical Quackery and Mr. St. John Long," 1 (1830), 451;
"Animal Magnetism," 1 (1830), 673; "The March of Intellect, and
Universal Education," 2 (1830–31), 161. See also Carlyle's own
"Schiller, Goethe and Madame de Stael" (*Fraser's*, 5 [1832], 171;
Works, 26:502) and his characterization of the age, after introduc-
tory remarks, in "Signs of the Times" (*Works*, 27:59), which was
published in the *Edinburgh Review*.

characterizing the age Carlyle used in his essays, "Burns" (*Works*, 26:258) and "German Playwrights" (*Works*, 26:355).

Our sense of the complexity and intention of the voice we hear in that first sentence is confirmed by the rest of the first chapter. The voice displays erudition, constant distrust of and sarcasm toward science, superb control of irony, and a tendency to use obscure historical references. He lists, for example, the accomplishments of science, then relegates them to the pantry and reduces them to the innocent wondering of Peter Pindar's George III: "To many a Royal Society, the Creation of a World is little more mysterious than the cooking of a dumpling; concerning which last, indeed, there have been minds to whom the question, *How the apples were got in*, presented difficulties" (p. 4, n). In fact, the allusiveness, the erudition of the Editor further associates *Sartor* with *Fraser's* and other contemporary periodicals. These were familiar qualities in essays with and without fictionalized persona published in these journals.[15]

What we learn about the Editor from his words in the first chapter determines how we interpret his statements about himself in the second chapter. When he says that he "is animated with a true though perhaps a feeble attachment to the Institutions of our Ancestors" and that no "personal connection of ours with Teufelsdröckh, Heuschrecke, or this Philosophy of Clothes, can pervert our judgment or sway us to extenuate or exaggerate" (p. 13), we tend to doubt his absolute sincerity, because we are already used to his speaking ironically, because

[15] See Michael Allen, "Learning and Journalism," *Poe and the British Magazine Tradition*, pp. 74–100.

we know, even by some of his revolutionary syntax, that he is a radical, and because we have seen him exaggerate. Critics have argued that the few statements the Editor makes about himself here in "Editorial Difficulties" reveal the assigned characteristics according to which he ought to behave in the rest of the book. This position is an impossible one because the Editor is not what he says he is. He takes an attitude toward science in absolute agreement with that of Teufelsdröckh and the implied orator, in a style distinguishable from Teufelsdröckh's only by its framework of neutral clauses put there to maintain the appearance of a distinction between the two. The Editor shows, if anything, greater verbal dexterity and powers of irony than Teufelsdröckh. He shows erudition and intelligence and eccentricities indistinguishable from the Professor's. As early as "Editorial Difficulties" he offers an extended simile in Teufelsdröckh's manner (p. 12; cf. p. 286). There is no point in talking about the Editor as a consistently represented character in a novel, the plot of which concerns a conflict between him and Teufelsdröckh or between him and German documents. The Editor is not consistently represented. If one wanted to argue that the Editor participated in such a plot, one would have to argue further that the plot is resolved, by agreement between the Editor and Teufelsdröckh, before the book begins.

The Editor's voice is a manifestation of the voice of the implied orator. The Editor may appear to be neutral or critical, as we have seen, but that neutrality is always qualified by our sense of the implied orator, just as the neutral elements of the first sentence of the book are qualified by the polemical elements. We are always aware of the presence of the implied orator, and a large part of our pleasure is in knowing that orator implicitly. We feel his presence with more and more confidence as the book progresses, and we enjoy watching the Editor or, less frequently, Teufelsdröckh, take positions at some distance from the implied orator, knowing that this is done to aid our understanding. The use of the particular fiction of the Editor has many rhetorical advantages. The Editor can reinforce the Clothes Philosophy by direct advocacy: "Wild as it looks, this Philosophy of Clothes, can we ever reach its real meaning, promises to reveal new-coming Eras, the first dim rudiments and already-budding germs of a nobler Era, in Universal History" (p. 80). He can ridicule in order to ease us into a careful evaluation: "Or again, has it often been the lot of our readers to read such stuff as we shall now quote?" (p. 44). He can express "astonishment" at Teufelsdröckh's views in order to accommodate certain of our fears (p. 249). In short, he can perform a wide variety of rhetorical operations which help advance the Clothes Philosophy.

Yet the Editor must place certain restrictions on what Carlyle can and cannot do and so determine to some degree the structure of the book. The limitations the Editor imposes are essentially those that the rest of Carlyle's fictional apparatus imposes, which will be discussed more fully in chapter 6 below. In order to maintain the conditions established at the outset of the book, the fiction of the Editor must be maintained. He may speak in a variety of ways, but what he says must be made, in itself or in its context, to agree with the Clothes Philosophy. And he may not be abandoned as a device. Not a great deal is required to keep up the pretense that an Editor is present, editing materials, but the pretense must be maintained or the reader will feel the consistency of the book has been violated. Furthermore, Carlyle cannot allow his readers to take the Editor seriously as a character who is developed consistently according to his assigned characteristics. If the Editor begins genuinely to oppose the Clothes Philosophy in such a way that he calls attention to himself and his troubles and away from the Clothes Philosophy, then, too, the reader will feel his natural, cumulative interest in the presentation of the Clothes Philosophy has been interrupted and that he is being lured out of a persuasive essay and into a fable.

The functions of the fictional voice of Teufelsdröckh are easier to grasp than those of the Editor, especially in Books First and Third. Teufelsdröckh is, according to the fiction, creating arguments about the nature of the world and the needs of its people, propagating the Clothes Philosophy. He has always been understood to be an advocate of the ideas that the implied orator is propagating, as he usually is. He is, like the Editor, a reflex of the persuasive argument of the whole book. Carlyle employs him to state his ideas in various ways, emphatically, hyperbolically, ironically, sarcastically, prophetically, any of which modes of speaking can be qualified or reinforced, as necessary, explicitly by the Editor or implicitly by the implied orator. The rhetorical advantages of these fictions are considerable. Carlyle can create certain effects consistent with his ideas. The truth can seem to come from a remote and sometimes inscrutable authority. The difficulty of knowing truth can be parodied by the apparent difficulty of making out what Teufelsdröckh means. The greatest advantages, however, are flexibility of tone and

also the creation of circumstances in which Carlyle can
do one thing while seeming to do another. The reader is
likely to be flattered at feeling he is sharing an intimacy
with the author unavailable to a duller, and probably non-
existent, reader who does not perceive the serious argument of the book. If he is not pleased, he will at least be
likely to admit the skill of a writer who can conduct a
serious argument while creating fictions that appear at
first to be doing only foolish things.

Without developing a complex psychology to explain
a man's creation and use of fictions or of their effects,[16]
we can see comprehensible reasons for his choosing the
particular fictions he does. The fictions provided rhetorical advantages, and they took advantage of Carlyle's
own experience and circumstances. The Editor is used, as
G. B. Tennyson has shown, to perform the activities of
"editor-translator, critic, reviewer, essayist," and "bio-
grapher," which Carlyle knew from his own literary experience up to 1830 (*Sartor Called Resartus*, p. 87).

The invention of Teufelsdröckh was natural enough as
well. The works Carlyle had reviewed, edited, criticized,
and translated had been primarily German, and his reputation depended on them. His invention of Teufelsdröckh
may have had an incidental stimulus in the form of Carlyle's friend Francis Jeffrey. The former editor of the
Edinburgh Review had just ended a visit at Craigenputtock when Carlyle wrote in his notebook that he was

[16] For an idea of what a psychology of the perceptions of fictions in nonfictional prose might be like, see Norman N. Holland,
"Prose and Minds: A Psychoanalytic Approach to Non-Fiction,"
in *The Art of Victorian Prose*, ed. George Levine and William
Madden, pp. 314–37.

about to begin "Nonsense."[17] David Alec Wilson points out that the two men had disagreed earlier about Carlyle's use in his "Burns" essay of what Jeffrey called "that very well used joke of the clothes making the man and the tailor being a creator" (D. A. Wilson, 2:73).[18] The two men had a more serious, long-standing disagreement over the value of German literature and "mysticism." Two months before his visit, for example, Jeffrey, inquiring about the progress of the *History of German Literature*, asked, "And is there any hope that the closer acquaintance into which it must have forced you with those muddyheaded, half crazy, half affected, and uniformly vulgar scribblers, will open your eyes to their true character, or disabuse you at least of your idolatrous admiration?" (D. A. Wilson, 2:158). By creating Teufelsdröckh and the Editor, Carlyle could play good naturedly on his own conviction that the Germans were a source of the truth he knew. He could indulge Jeffrey and an English audience, who would read about any subject but German literature,[19] in a tolerant laugh at the idea that the German from his tower could "tell the Universe, which so often forgets that fact, what o'clock it really is" (*Sartor*, p. 6).[20]

[17] D. A. Wilson, 2, 180–82; *TN*, pp. 173–76.

[18] See also Maxwell H. Goldberg, "Jeffrey: Mutilator of Carlyle's 'Burns'?" *PMLA*, 56 (1941), 466–71.

[19] In refusing to print Carlyle's *History of German Literature*, the publisher Tait wrote Carlyle on 29 July 1830 that he would be "proud to publish for you again, upon almost any subject but German Literature." Recent books on that subject had failed, and "the feeling in the public mind is that anything German is most especially to be avoided" (D. A. Wilson, 2:159).

[20] Carlyle's reputation made the German qualities of *Sartor* less a disguise than they appear today. Even in America an anonymous reviewer in "Thomas Carlyle," *New York Review*, 4 (1839), said

There were more profound reasons for the invention of
Teufelsdröckh as well. With this fictional device Carlyle
could gain, when he desired it, a kind of authority he felt
was his but was not available to him in his own name. He
had no "books" of his own, no basis for speaking in his
own voice, if he had one, with the authority he felt belonged to him. Though he had published a great deal,
he felt he was not properly recognized. In August 1830
he had received communication from the Saint-Simonians
in Paris, directed to the author of "Signs of the Times."[21]
He wrote to his mother, "The people there seem to think
me a very promising man, and that some good will come
of me. Thus, a prophet is not without honour, save in his
own country. Poor prophet! However, in my present soli-
tude, I am very glad of these small encouragements" (*Letters*, 1:226). In his own country Carlyle was something
of a foreigner, a feeling bound to be accentuated by his
Scottish heritage. Using the role of a German prophet
was natural and took advantage of his position. In December 1828 he had written to Eckermann: "For you must
know that I pass here generally enough for a 'mystic'
or man half-drowned in the abysses of German speculation; which, considering everything, is all, in my opinion,

---

that *Sartor* "appeared without the author's name, but was known
by all to be from the Anglo-Germanic head and heart of Thomas
Carlyle" (p. 179).

[21] For the influence of the Saint-Simonians see Hill Shine, *Carlyle and the Saint-Simonians: The Concept of Historical Periodicity* (Baltimore: Johns Hopkins Press, 1941); René Wellek, "Carlyle
and the Philosophy of History," *PQ*, 23 (1944), 55–76; and Richard
Kier Pethick Pankhurst, *The Saint-Simonians, Mill, and Carlyle:
A Preface to Modern Thought* (London: Sidgwick and Jackson,
1957).

exactly as it should be."[22] In employing in an exaggerated fashion a role that was assigned to him and that in a profound way genuinely was his, he saw the possibility of accomplishing his persuasive purpose. The fictional devices of Teufelsdröckh and the Editor allowed him to achieve a significant measure of success.

[22] Quoted by William A. Speck, "New Letters of Carlyle to Eckermann," *Yale Review*, 15 (July 1926), 740.

4: Intuition Quickened by Experience

> Experience, often repeated, perhaps a certain instinct of something far deeper that lies under such experience, has taught men so much.
>
> CARLYLE, "CHARACTERISTICS"[1]

In Books First and Third the thread of Carlyle's argument may be relatively clear because what he pretends to do, trace Teufelsdröckh's ideas, is coordinated with what he is actually doing, arguing for the Clothes Philosophy. Book Second may be more difficult to penetrate. There, what he appears to do, write a biography of Teufelsdröckh, seems less related to what he has been doing, to what he has engaged our interest in. Book Second, is, nonetheless, consistent with the other two Books and necessary to them and to Carlyle's whole argument. Through this biography Carlyle gives Teufelsdröckh's voice and indirectly the implied orator's the authority of experience, by reiterating a process of insight that leads to crucial elements of the Clothes Philosophy, and by reinforcing constantly different elements of this set of ideas. The Clothes Philosophy springs from kinds of experience, intuitive and felt. Book Second attempts to perform the difficult task of making that experience intelligible and available to the reader. Carlyle does so by a

[1] *Works*, 28:17.

variety of examples and arguments, by trying at times to recreate in the reader the kind of experience that leads to the Clothes Philosophy. Because it provides as essential justification for the premises of the Clothes Philosophy and for many of Carlyle's conclusions, it is a necessary part of *Sartor*.

The use of Book Second as a gloss on Carlyle's own life has obscured its relationship to the rest of *Sartor*. The purpose of Book Second, however, is not autobiographical, "expressive" in that sense.[2] The number of actual correlations between Teufelsdröckh's life and Carlyle's does suggest that he saw elements of his own experience as an authority for his ideas.[3] A striking fact is that Book

[2] In *English Autobiography: Its Emergence, Materials, and Form*, University of California English Studies, 8 (Berkeley: Univ. of California Press, 1954), Wayne Shumaker remarks that Book Second of *Sartor* is important to an understanding of Carlyle's intellectual development, but that Teufelsdröckh has experiences that Carlyle did not have: "He sees the Great Wall of China, serves the Emperor Napoleon, is nearly shot as a spy. More important still, *Sartor* was not given to the public as 'truth,' but as something else—what, we need not now determine" (pp. 104–05).

[3] Alexander Carlyle has shown that, when Froude quoted Carlyle as saying that "Nothing in *Sartor Resartus* is fact; symbolical myth all, except that of the incident in the Rue St. Thomas de l'Enfer," Froude misquoted Carlyle. See Appendix B, *The Love Letters of Thomas Carlyle and Jane Welsh*, ed. Alexander Carlyle (London: John Lane, 1909), II, 365–66. Carlyle's actual statements were made in reference to specific passages in *Sartor*, and they do not exclude as many details or "facts" as Froude's misquotation suggests. Alexander Carlyle, with this justification, goes on to list details in *Sartor* that seem to correspond with details of Carlyle's life (*Love Letters*, 2:367–87). Some of the parallels are quite convincing. Teufelsdröckh is born in Entepfuhl, or Duck Pond. Ecclefechan, Carlyle's birthplace, possessed a prominent duck pond. Teufelsdröckh's mother's name is Gretchen, the German diminutive, as Alexander Carlyle points out, of Margaret, the name of

Second has been taken to be autobiographical independent of any such knowledge of Carlyle's life. Joseph
Hartwell Barrett remarked in 1849 that the work becomes
a satire on modern civilization "from the author's identifying himself with his subject—and, in fact, as most
readers at once infer, from having himself passed through
the very series of experiences here attributed to his hero"
("Sartor Resartus," p. 121). The contention that Book
Second is autobiographical seems frequently to be based
on inference or at the most on inference with a minimum
of external support. This is true even in the case of a mind
as acute as Ernst Cassirer's. Discussing the "autobiographical element" in Carlyle's philosophy, he says, citing
no external evidence, that "there can be no doubt of the
authenticity" of the scene described in "The Everlasting
No."[4] The long history of the use of *Sartor* as a gloss on
Carlyle's innermost life seems to be based on exactly this
kind of inference. In fact only recently has it been shown
in what way the "incident in the Rue St. Thomas de
l'Enfer," which Carlyle sanctioned as accurate, is related
to Carlyle's actual experience. Carlisle Moore has shown
that this important incident as it appears in *Sartor* does
not correspond to one single incident in Carlyle's life, that

---

Carlyle's mother. Carlyle himself acknowledged the similarities
between his schooling and the Professor's. Other parallels, especially the whole matter of the similarities between Blumine, Teufelsdröckh's young love, and Margaret Gordon, a girl Carlyle knew
briefly in 1818, are less compelling and even misleading (*Love Letters*, 2:387–430). On the whole, the quantity of parallels does show
that Carlyle had elements of his experience in mind as a justification for his ideas.

[4] Cassirer, "The Preparation: Carlyle," in *The Myth of the State*
(New Haven: Yale Univ. Press, 1946), p. 198. Cited as *Myth*.

is, that it does not represent an actual conversion in Leith Walk, as it had traditionally been held to.[5] Carlyle compressed a process of conversion that took place over a period of time for precise, dramatic effect. The Everlasting No represents a process of thought that is autobiographical, but not in such a way that it could be considered true autobiography. Since Book Second is shaped so perfectly to support the ideas of the implied orator, one might naturally suspect that the experiences outlined there were the author's. This supposition, however, can only be checked by outside evidence, an one cannot deduce properly from the text that it necessarily represents the author's experience. That Carlyle could take elements of his own experience, shape them into something freshly imagined and coherent in order to support his ideas, and convince readers that the experience was actual is a tribute to his skill.

Through Hofrath Heuschrecke and the Editor, Carlyle tends to discourage any reading of Book Second as an allegory of his autobiography. When the Hofrath wishes to impress on the Editor the importance of a biography of Teufelsdröckh, he says, as the Editor quotes him, " 'Nay,' adds he, 'were the speculative scientific Truth even known, you still, in this inquiring age, ask yourself, Whence came it, and Why, and How?—and rest not, till, if no better may be, Fancy have shaped-out an answer; and either in the authentic lineaments of Fact, or the forged ones of Fiction, a complete picture and Genetical History of the Man and his spiritual Endeavour lies before you' " (p. 75). The Hofrath says that the mind is not

[5] *"Sartor Resartus* and the Problem of Carlyle's 'Conversion,' " *PMLA*, 70 (1955), 662–81.

satisfied with abstract truth but must know that truth
for itself in human terms. It does not matter whether
"Fancy," or the imagination, recreates the biography of
the speaker of this truth out of fact or fiction, as long as
the product satisfies. Carlyle feels that the mind must
recreate the experiences and intuitions that led to a set
of ideas before they can be accepted, and he hopes to
perform this process for the reader in Book Second. He
suggests again at the end of Book Second that it should
not be taken as literal autobiography. The Editor airs a
suspicion that he has not been dealing with facts in
making Teufelsdröckh's biography: "What if many a so-
called Fact were little better than a Fiction; if here we had
no direct Camera-obscura Picture of the Professor's History; but only some more or less fantastic Adumbration,
symbolically, perhaps significantly enough, shadowing-
forth the same!" (p. 202). He then quotes Teufelsdröckh
disparaging "Facts" as a way of knowing a man. The
meaning of a man's life is something available in coherent
form to the imagination and is not necessarily based on
fact. In Carlyle's sense, then, but not in the common one,
Sartor may be a better biography of Carlyle than anyone
else will ever write. And we should be sufficiently warned
not to try to read biographical "fact" from *Sartor*.

If Book Second is not autobiography in a conventional
sense, it still gives the appearance of being a form of narrative.[6] In this Book, however, Carlyle constantly moves
from a specific to a generalized representation, then to a
more direct mode of address. Representation turns to a

[6] MacMechan, for example, calls it a novel surrounded by appendixes, and G. B. Tennyson calls it a "Märchen" (*Sartor Called
Resartus*, esp. pp. 79, 190).

purer form of rhetoric, and the fictions are manipulated
to exhort the reader directly. In effect, Carlyle turns to
address the reader, and the reader is, at least intuitively,
aware of it. We are moved initially and at times thereafter out of incipient sympathy and concern for the fate
of Teufelsdröckh, as we might be in a novel or other form
of narrative. As we are shown the implications of what
is being represented, however, our interest broadens. Our
concern is more and more constantly shifted from the
specific individual and his fate to the implications themselves and their effect on us. Finally we are aware that we
are being addressed directly, shown and exhorted to abide
by the implications of what has become a form of argument. Perhaps the directness with which Carlyle speaks,
especially at the close of Book Second, accounts for the
dislike many lovers of fable, or narrative fiction, have for
Sartor.

Book Second is not, then, simple representation or narrative. Yet it may be argued that a description of it as in
outline fictional biography designed to support a set of
ideas appears to be a description of an apologue or "exemplum."[7] The essential difference between an apologue
or exemplum and Book Second lies in Carlyle's use of
narrative as a base for exhortation. We are more aware
of a voice speaking out of experience and interpreting it
than we are of the experience itself, of its representation.
The experience itself is represented only as much as is
necessary to allow the "implied orator" to speak out of it
with sufficient authority to make the Clothes Philosophy
believable as a product of experience. What is spoken is

[7] G. B. Tennyson calls Book Second an "exemplum" (*Sartor
Called Resartus,* p. 291).

the sign of profound and mysterious experience, but the experience itself is never allowed ascendancy over the Clothes Philosophy. Book Second is, then, different from conventional apologues or exempla in that what is learned from experience is explicit in Book Second and the experience is often implicit, while in most apologues the experience is explicit and what is learned generally implicit. Essentially the same argument may be made against Book Second as a part of a novel or other form of narrative fiction. In "William Empson, Contemporary Criticism, and Poetic Diction," Elder Olson distinguishes between "*lexis* and *praxis*; between speech as meaningful and speech as action" (*Critics and Criticism*, p. 33). In Book Second Teufelsdröckh's speech about himself and the Editor's comments are primarily *lexis*, or speech that is meaningful and accountable, as Olson says, "in grammatical and lexicographical terms," and minimally *praxis*, or speech that is meaningful in terms of action, of situation and character. From Book Second we learn more about the Clothes Philosophy, and what we learn about its fictional creator bears only on his ideas.

Book Second is, then, part of a persuasive essay, designed to expand the Clothes Philosophy and give certain elements of it the authority of experience. It is not autobiography, though it is autobiographical in ways that would be difficult to test, and the reader is warned not to read it as fact. Book Second is, further, not simple representation, not a form of novel, exemplum, or other form of narrative fiction. One interest is primarily in the ideas presented and the voice presenting them.

Book Second is placed where it is to give the reader a sense of the speaker's authority, his ethos. It also strives to give the reader a maximum sense of the personal and historical implications of the Clothes Philosophy and to stir him to action. In an important way the personal and historical implications of the Clothes Philosophy are the same. Teufelsdröckh's life is linked to the lives of all men of Carlyle's generation, in a common ethos. The pattern he follows, "through the various successive states and stages of Growth, Entanglement, Unbelief, and almost Reprobation, into a certain clearer state of what he himself seems to consider as Conversion" (p. 198), is one that all young men do or should follow. Carlyle saw history itself in terms of biography and saw in certain lives representative patterns that may be imitated in the course of history or in individual lives.[8] For Carlyle, Goethe is the most important example. His progress from *Werther* to the *Wanderjahre* represented: "A change from inward imprisonment, doubt and discontent, into freedom, belief, and clear activity: such a change as, in our opinion must take place, more or less consciously, in every character that, especially in these times, attains to spiritual manhood" ("Goethe," *Works*, 26:243). Measured against Goethe, Byron falls short: "Byron was almost the only man we saw faithfully and manfully struggling, to the end, in this cause; and he dies while the victory was still doubtful, or at best, only beginning to be gained" (*ibid.*).

Any man's life has the additional effect of stirring us to active sympathy: "A poetic interest still more: for precisely this same struggle of human Freewill against material Necessity, which every man's Life, by the mere

[8] For a good discussion of this point and especially Carlyle's use of and attitude toward Byron, see Charles Richard Sanders, "The Byron Closed in *Sartor Resartus*," *SIR*, 3 (1964), 77–108.

circumstance that the man continues alive, will more or less victoriously exhibit,—is that which above all else, or rather inclusive of all else, calls the Sympathy of mortal hearts into action" ("Biography," *Works*, 28:44–45). The analogy early critics noticed between Book Second and "spiritual autobiography" is partially valid. Book Second presents in part a pattern of struggle and triumph that may be imitated, but the pattern is not a ritual Puritan one.[9] It has unique historical and social implications, and the subject ends up not only saved but exhorting others to the same state. Thus Teufelsdröckh's biography embodies and shapes the progress of a generation.[10]

To move the community along the proper spiritual course is no easy matter, however. Carlyle gains great persuasive power by focusing on the intuitional experience of his hero and making it both believable and sufficiently generalized to remain applicable to the lives of

[9] See William Haller, *The Rise of Puritanism: Or, The Way to the New Jerusalem as Set Forth in Pulpit and Press from Thomas Cartwright to John Lilburne and John Milton, 1570–1643* (New York: Columbia Univ. Press, 1938), p. 108, for an outline of the pattern of spiritual autobiographies. See also G. A. Starr, *Defoe and Spiritual Autobiography* (Princeton: Princeton Univ. Press, 1965).

[10] Roger Sharrock in "Carlyle and the Sense of History," *E&S*, 19 (1966), remarks that "Teufelsdröckh is the idealized essence of all the German thought and poetry Carlyle had met in books and of its creators, a sort of composite Goethe-Schiller-Richter youth, a *schöne Seele*" (pp. 86–87). He is also a Byron-Burns-Dr. Johnson and a Carlyle. See also the discussions of the multiple personalities in Teufelsdröckh in R. D. McMaster, "Criticism of Civilization in the Structure of *Sartor Resartus*," and in Eugene Goodheart, "Goethe, Carlyle, and 'The Sorrows of Werther,'" in *The Cult of the Ego: The Self in Modern Literature* (Chicago: Univ. of Chicago Press, 1968), pp. 61–89.

his generation and to the reader, even to a modern reader, whose world is not so unlike Carlyle's. The spiritual course is outlined in the series of experiences Teufelsdröckh passes through. It is necessary that it be outlined in this way because of the particular nature of belief for Carlyle. Teufelsdröckh and all men learn by intuition quickened by experience.[11] In order to make the reader ready to act on the Clothes Philosophy, Carlyle must lead him, as well as he can, through the intuitional experiences that get him to that state. Following Teufelsdröckh, with the aid of the Editor and the older Teufelsdröckh, achieves this for the reader.

Carlyle makes explicit the reasons for biography as well as the demands placed on the reader. When Hofrath Heuschrecke sends the Editor the mysterious bags full of biographical fragments, he reminds him of "what we knew well already," that "no Life-Philosophy (*Lebensphilosophie*), such as this of Clothes pretends to be, which originates equally in the character (*Gemüth*), and equally speaks thereto, can attain its significance till the Character itself is known and seen; 'till the Author's View of the World (*Weltansicht*), and how he actively and passively came by such view, are clear: in short till a Biography of him has been philosophico-poetically written, and philosophico-poetically read' " (p. 75). Heuschrecke also quotes Goethe's remark that "Man is properly the only object that interests man" (p. 75). Teufelsdröckh's ideas cannot have "significance" until the proper biog-

[11] The phrase "intuition quickened by experience," which is also the title of my chapter, is from Carlyle's summary of Book First, Chapter VIII, and is a description of Teufelsdröckh's method (*Sartor*, p. 51).

raphy of him is written and read. It must be read, as well
as written, because "significance" is not inert but active
and depends on the reader as well as on the writer. The
philosopher comes to his ideas "actively and passively,"
by intuition quickened by experience, and the reader must
follow the same process. The biography itself must be
"philosophico-poetically" written, must combine thought
and feeling without strict attention to "Fact" (p. 75), as
mentioned above, and must be "philosophico-poetically"
read in order to attain its "significance."

There is a notion lurking in criticism of *Sartor* that the
book is disordered as a result of the disorder of Carlyle's
mind, or at least of his processes of thought. This view
is stated in its extreme by Herbert J. C. Grierson who
compares Carlyle with the Hebrew prophets, in contrast
with those "whose thoughts are developed by a conscious
process of reasoning." Carlyle is a writer "who reaches
his conclusions by what we call intuition, whose imagination brooding over the course of things, or the flow of
consciousness within, reaches and declares the findings
which he, no more than those to whom or for whom he
speaks, can trace the steps by which they have been attained to and which are accepted, if accepted at all, by a
similar intuitional response."[12] Carlyle would undoubtedly be pleased to be put with such company. In fact,
he takes some pains to suggest that the process of intuition in which he engages is as mysterious and unique as
that which Grierson describes. But Carlyle does not fish
broodingly in the stream of consciousness, yanking out
what takes his bait. The process of intuition he describes

[12] "Thomas Carlyle," Annual Lecture on a Master Mind, *Proc.
British Acad.*, 26 (1940), 302.

and urges the reader to participate in is orderly, certainly retraceable—unless we take *Sartor* as the act of intuition itself—and perfectly intelligible. Carlyle's grasp of normal human experience is quite firm, and the sequence of intuitions he presents in Book Second is perfectly comprehensible. The reader of *Sartor* need not be a Hebrew prophet himself to understand, though he may be flattered by Carlyle's attempts to make him feel he is one.

The Clothes Philosophy is enforced at every point. The very nature of the biography of Teufelsdröckh, fragments in six paper bags (pp. 77–78),[13] which must be deciphered, mirrors Carlyle's notion of a symbolic universe that must be read and ordered by the mind. This fictional device of edited fragments also permits a sophisticated range of commentary on Teufelsdröckh's life. The Editor can comment or summarize, taking a convenient posture. Teufelsdröckh, the mature man, can comment on his own past or can recreate his own voice speaking directly out of his youthful experience. And Teufelsdröckh, the growing young man, can speak about his present experience. The flexibility of narration Carlyle gains allows him to control very precisely the reader's awareness and understanding of Teufelsdröckh's experience and ultimately to move the reader directly into the process of reasoning or intuition that resolves itself in the Clothes Philosophy.[14] All the while the resolution of this series of in-

[13] See G. B. Tennyson's discussion of fragments, *Sartor Called Resartus*, pp. 223–27.

[14] The device of an older man narrating and commenting on his youthful adventures in a novel is, of course, a familiar one. But the effects achieved by Carlyle are very different from those achieved by Dickens, for example, in *David Copperfield*. David broods over his childhood, governing our responses to and our understanding

sights is readily available in the voice of the mature Teufelsdröckh and occasionally of the Editor, minimizing suspense but maximizing comprehension and belief.

The conventions governing the progress of Book Second are superficially those of biography. Although "in a psychological point of view, it is perhaps questionable whether from birth and geneology, how closely scrutinized soever, much insight is to be gained" (p. 81), men are still naturally curious about the births of great men. Thus Carlyle, like most biographers, begins at the Beginning. Teufelsdröckh is left to Andreas Futteral, a former soldier, "a man of order, courage, downrightness" (p. 83), fit to prepare his ward in limited fashion for the warfare of life. The Professor's first appearance is appropriately mysterious, perhaps even supernatural, though the Editor drops a plain suggestion that it may be perfectly natural (p. 89).

The fiction of the fragments allows Carlyle to force the reader to associate himself with Teufelsdröckh and to take a particular attitude toward his own birth. The Editor includes the following fragment: " 'And yet, O Man born of Woman,' cries the Autobiographer, with one of his sudden whirls, 'wherein is my case peculiar? Hadst thou, any more than I, a Father whom thou know-

---

of the child's situation and controlling also our expectations about the kind of maturity the boy must achieve in order for the plot to be resolved. In *Sartor*, however, we are concerned for full understanding of a set of ideas and not for the fate of a character, except as the fate of the character will aid our understanding. Teufelsdröckh's specific situation becomes more and more obscure as Book Second progresses. Imagine David's fading into the background in the last several chapters of *Copperfield* and Dickens's exhorting us all to do our duty.

est? The Andreas and Gretchen, or the Adam and Eve, who led thee into Life, and for a time suckled and pap-fed thee there, whom thou namest Father and Mother; these were, like mine, but thy nursing-father and nursing-mother: thy true Beginning and Father is in Heaven, whom with the bodily eye thou shalt never behold, but only with the spiritual' " (p. 86). Any anxiety the reader may have about his own worth is to be calmed by aware-ness of the divine parentage he shares with Teufels-dröckh. Such explicit attempts to associate the reader with Teufelsdröckh occur throughout Book Second. They are similar to the Editor's attempts to stir the reader to activity out of concern for his own fate, and they control our attitudes toward Teufelsdröckh. We accept him as less extraordinary than we did before. But, even in order to do so, we are led directly to change our attitudes toward ourselves and to believe in another aspect of the Clothes Philosophy.

Similarly, Teufelsdröckh's subsequent account of his own naming works on our ideas as well as on our judgment of Teufelsdröckh, for names "are the most important of all Clothings" (p. 87). Here as usual, Teufelsdröckh operates within the world of the Clothes Philosophy and not within the world of common ex-perience which fills the traditional novel. Critics have noticed in *Sartor* the lack of circumstantial detail found in novels. These are absent precisely because they are not important to the kind of spiritual, intuitive experience Carlyle is trying to persuade us to participate in. The external world matters initially as only a barrier to self-realization, a negative stimulus to further perception, and ultimately as something to be worked upon by the individual and collective will. The external world is, after all, only superficial clothing. Lack of conventional novelistic detail does not by itself signify a lack of novelistic organization. But Teufelsdröckh operates in the world of the Clothes Philosophy only in order to make the reader believe in and act by that set of ideas, not finally as a character in a represented action about whose fate we are made to care. Potential concern for Teufelsdröckh's fate is expanded into concern for our own fates and the resolution of certain intellectual and spiritual difficulties in our own minds. This complex operation needs more explanation.

Teufelsdröckh's experience is primarily visual, literally and metaphorically. He grows by a succession of insights and intuitions. As a youngster he is somewhat given to philosophizing. He sees in swine (p. 93) and birds (p. 96) lessons in social organization. When he does so, we are aware intuitively of the extent to which *lexis*, language as meaning, rules over *praxis*, language as action, in Book Second. What the boy says reveals his character; it is an action with certain implications. But the implications of what he says are not to be taken very seriously or profoundly as an indication of character. We do not feel when the boy speaks with wisdom beyond his years, as a grown Teufelsdröckh in terms perfectly compatible with his mature beliefs, that we are gaining insight into a prodigy, as extraordinary as this boy is supposed to be. We recognize the artificiality of his being made to speak this way and apprehend what he says primarily as *lexis*, as meaning. We understand that, indeed, there may be lessons in social organization in swine and birds.

Carlyle's representation of Teufelsdröckh is often more

complex. He is not represented in every case simply as a diminutive prophet who speaks truth. He is represented as passing through a series of increasingly intense insights, in which his speech approaches speech as action, but is restricted carefully by dense commentary so that our interest is in ideas, not in individual character, situation, action. In fact Carlyle attempts to draw *lexis* and *praxis* together, to make speech as meaning and speech as action inseparable. That is, he attempts to make his character speak words that reveal his character, his situation, and something about the actions in which he is involved, and which are also true, are pure meaning. This attempt makes for rather portentous talk. Little remains implicit. Elder Olson points out the immense power as *praxis* of Lear's apparently innocuous remark, "Pray you, undo this button" (*Critics and Criticism*, p. 50). But Carlyle uses the individual as a way of talking about the community and does not choose to do so by isolating his one figure Teufelsdröckh. At one point Teufelsdröckh is unaccommodated himself and the elder Teufelsdröckh recalls, "I was alone, alone!" This statement is *praxis*, a simple statement like Lear's with innumerable implications which depend on our knowledge of and predisposition to sympathize with his predicament. But Teufelsdröckh continues in a manner that focuses on pure meaning and turns to implicit exhortation: "Ever too the strong inward longing shaped Fantasms for itself: toward these, one after the other, must I fruitlessly wander. A feeling I had, that for my fever-thirst there was and must be somewhere a Healing Fountain. To many fondly imagined Fountains, the Saints' Wells of these days, did I pilgrim; to great Men, to great Cities, to great Events:

but found there no healing" (p. 154). The search becomes a search for meaning which itself reveals meanings. Longing shapes "Fantasms." The longing cannot be satisfied by the best civilization affords. Carlyle would like us to feel Teufelsdröckh embodies all longing young men of his generation, the whole of the youthful world, in action, which is the only source of meaning. He would like us to feel this with the same intensity and quality of feeling we may have for an individual, for a Lear. Though he succeeds to a remarkable extent, he does not do so fully, partly because of the density of commentary needed to keep the full meaning and implications of Teufelsdröckh's position before us.[15] What is lost in intensity and particularization of feeling is made up in increased understanding of ideas, of the predicament of a whole generation, which is our real, lasting interest.[16] The reader perceives that the fundamental action is Carlyle's act of exhorting the reader, not the action in which Teufelsdröckh appears to be involved. Book Second remains an essay and does not become dramatic action, does not be-

[15] Imagine the effect on *King Lear* if the ghost of Lear and the director of the play constantly leapt out of the wings to explain the meaning of Lear's actions and the relationship of his situation to that of all fathers and kings of his time and if Lear himself always understood and articulated fully his predicament, coming to the same judgments the audience, his ghost, and the director came to. The representation of Lear's situation would be replaced by a kind of three-way speech about a historical, social, and personal problem, or a one-way speech in three voices. The play would become a theatrical essay or rhetorical display, which could hardly be called a play.

[16] That our real interest is in ideas is reemphasized by Carlyle at the end of Book Second. The Editor asks to review "what our degree of progress, during these Ten Chapters, has been, toward right understanding of the *Clothes-Philosophy*" (pp. 204–05).

come a novel or other form of narrative representation.

The full implications of Teufelsdröckh's situation are kept before us, so that we are very much aware of a progress of ideas. Early Teufelsdröckh recognizes "the ring of Necessity." The mature Teufelsdröckh adds the comment: "Happy he for whom a kind heavenly Sun brightens it into a ring of Duty," which as Harrold's note suggests, anticipates again the gospel of work in "The Everlasting Yea" (pp. 97–98 n). Through such commentary the inevitable conclusion of Teufelsdröckh's insights is kept before us. The boy's father dies while he is in school, and this normally traumatic experience is treated only as a lesson: "the inexorable word, NEVER! now first showed its meaning" (p. 106). His mother then "revealed" his birth to him: "A certain poetic elevation, yet also a corresponding civic depression, it naturally imparted: *I was like no other*; in which fixed-idea, leading sometimes to highest, and oftener to frightfullest results, may there not lie the first spring of tendencies, which in my Life have become remarkable enough?" (p. 107). Carlyle succeeds in arousing a certain amount of interest in the fate of this unique and mysterious young man, but not much suspense. We are always told what he will develop into, what his "tendencies" are; but we still wish to know how he will develop, for his sake and for the consequences the path he takes has for us. Yet, though our attention may be focused on Teufelsdröckh as an individual momentarily, he is never made our exclusive interest.

His love affair, which we would expect to be most individual, is an historic one and intentionally so. He enters it a young Romantic and leaves it an ideal Victorian, idealizing women, but impervious to their power, free ultimately of Wertherian suicidal tendencies and Byronic guilt: "To the Professor, women are henceforth Pieces of Art; of Celestial Art, indeed; which celestial pieces he glories to survey, but has lost thought of purchasing" (p. 135). But Blumine is not relegated with the rest of her sex to the status of Victorian furniture, to be bought and sold, without exacting a toll on Teufelsdröckh's stability. The immediate external world of experience has real effects on spiritual progress, and it cannot be simply denied.

Teufelsdröckh spiritualizes his attraction to her from the start, but his language suggests recognizable, frustrated human passion:

Without doubt, some Angel, whereof so many hovered round, would one day, leaving "the outskirts of *Æsthetic Tea*," flit nigher; and, by electric Promethean glance, kindle no despicable firework. Happy, if it indeed proved a Firework, and flamed-off rocket-wise, in successive beautiful bursts of splendour, each growing naturally from the other, through the several stages of a happy Youthful Love; till the whole were safely burnt-out; and the young soul relieved with little damage! Happy, if it did not rather prove a Conflagration and mad Explosion; painfully lacerating the heart itself; nay perhaps bursting the heart in pieces (which were Death); or at best, bursting the thin walls of your "reverberating furnace," so that it rage thenceforth all unchecked among the contiguous combustibles (which were Madness): till of the so fair and manifold internal world of our Diogenes, there remained Nothing or only the "crater of an extinct Volcano"!

[p. 134]

Teufelsdröckh is not to be sacrificed to orgastic passion. Carlyle directs our attention to the insight gained as a result of this experience, but at the same time he lets us

know, especially as Teufelsdröckh gets closer to the
Everlasting Yea, that the experience that quickens intuition is real and potentially damaging, in spite of his occasional statements that the individual will shapes a plastic
reality. As the Editor says, "Psychological readers are not
without curiosity to see how Teufelsdröckh, in this for
him unexampled predicament, demeans himself" (p.
135). The apparent Eden of Blumine's company is felici-
tous, but the mature Teufelsdröckh warns that in love
"Fantasy . . . superadds itself to sight" and makes love
similar to insanity (p. 141). Teufelsdröckh's predicament
is constantly located, generalized by the elder Teufelsdröckh and by the Editor. The reader is constantly told the
meaning of what happens at the expense of the action
itself. In a famous remark, the Editor points to the conventionality of his position when Blumine deserts him.
Teufelsdröckh, says the Editor, "has only one of three
things which he can next do: Establish himself in Bedlam; begin writing Satanic Poetry; or blow-out his
brains" (p. 146).

When Blumine chooses a richer man, he is left "a hap-
less air-navigator, plunging amid torn parachutes, sand-
bags, and confused wreck, fast enough into the jaws of
the Devil!" (p. 145). But he is without any bearings; his
"Morning-star" is dimmed and become a "Portent, an-
nouncing that the Doomsday had dawned!" (p. 145). The
religious language surrounding Teufelsdröckh's romance
helps enforce the point that young love is falsely directed
worship: " 'It was a Calenture,' adds he, 'whereby the
Youth saw green Paradise-groves in the waste Ocean-
waters: a lying vision, yet not wholly a lie, for *he* saw

it' " (pp. 147–48). Romantic love is a stage to be passed beyond, but a real stage nonetheless.[17]

Our feelings about Teufelsdröckh's spiritual state are controlled in part by metaphors. Teufelsdröckh is a sailor with no bearings, a man of vision who cannot see, and even a "wounded eagle" (p. 149). Each of these states is one we hope to see corrected. The visual metaphor is a dominating one and is used with variety and richness to suggest the presence or threat of disorder and confusion in Teufelsdröckh's mind during his wanderings. In a subtle and moving way Teufelsdröckh's health of mind and spiritual progress are linked with the states of the world we feel most profoundly, night and day, storm and fair weather, order or disorder in the immediate environment.

The orderliness of a landscape seems to bring stability, "Peace," to Teufelsdröckh: "To Peace, however, in this vortex of existence, can the Son of Time not pretend: Still less if some Spectre haunt him from the Past; and

[17] In "Voltaire," written in the spring of 1829, Carlyle said, "Woman, it has been sufficiently demonstrated, was given to man as a benefit, and for mutual support; a precious ornament and staff whereupon to lean in many trying situations" (*Works*, 26:434). The Blumine incident is clearly an attempt, a sympathetic one, to turn the attention of young men away from the distractions of romantic love, which is itself made to appear the misapplication or misdirection of philosophical or spiritual feeling, not plain human passion. Cf. his ridiculing of the idea that Novalis' career could have been shaped by the death of his young love (*Works*, 27:15–16). Carlyle seems to have understood passion, but he clearly felt that it should be of less significance than it often assumed in young lives, or in romantic conventions of the day; see the story, "The Wounded Spirit," by D. M. Moir, which appeared in the early numbers of *Fraser's* (1 [1830], 417–26, 663–72; 2 [1830–31], 397–411).

the Future is wholly a Stygian Darkness, spectre-bearing" (p. 150). But Nature triumphs, calling his attention out to the mountains: "He gazed over those stupendous masses with wonder, almost with longing desire; never till this hour had he known Nature, that she was One, that she was his Mother and divine" (p. 151). But neither Teufelsdröckh nor the reader is allowed to rest on this discovery.

Through the landscape trots Blumine in her wedding carriage with Towgood, Teufelsdröckh's former friend. Teufelsdröckh is left quoting Richter, *"I remained alone, behind them, with the Night"* (p. 151). Carlyle makes us feel, however, that this disruption of what seemed for a moment to be order in Teufelsdröckh's life is desirable. The Editor digs out a quotation from the mature Teufelsdröckh condemning the romantic stance he has taken as a youth among the mountains: " 'Some time before Small-pox was extirpated,' says the Professor, 'there came a new malady of the spiritual sort on Europe: I mean the epidemic, now endemical, of View-hunting' " (p. 151). Teufelsdröckh adds, "Never, as I compute, till after the *Sorrows of Werter*, was there man found who would say: Come let us make a Description! Having drunk the liquor, come let us eat the glass! Of which endemic the Jenner is unhappily still to seek" (p. 152). Again, Carlyle forces us to recognize we are dealing with historical and social problems, not simply personal ones. By forcing the reader to see that Teufelsdröckh's attitudes and behavior are rooted in social and historical conventions, not just conventions of individual psychology and character, Carlyle keeps the reader's attention on what he has been interested in from the beginning of

Sartor, on the meaning and implications for him of the Clothes Philosophy.

At this point Teufelsdröckh begins his wanderings, and Carlyle modifies the kind of biography he presents:

In figurative language, we might say he becomes, not indeed a spirit, yet spiritualised, vaporised. Fact unparalleled in Biography: The river of his History, which we have traced from its tiniest fountains, and hoped to see flow onward, with increasing current, into the ocean, here dashes itself over that terrific Lover's Leap; and, as a mad-foaming cataract, flies wholly into tumultuous clouds of spray! Low down it indeed collects again into pools and plashes; yet only at a great distance, and with difficulty, if at all, into a general stream. To cast a glance into certain of those pools and plashes, and trace whither they run, must, for a chapter or two, form the limit of our endeavour.

[p. 153]

This figure allows Carlyle to drop the chronological narrative he has established. It also allows him to neglect, even more than he has, circumstantial aspects of experience. Teufelsdröckh becomes pure mind and spirit. Our perception of Teufelsdröckh moves even farther from perception of him as an individual. More explicit efforts are made to have us associate Teufelsdröckh with broader spiritual progress, with the whole Romantic movement as it extends and is modified, past Byron to Goethe. We become interested more explicitly in what the implied orator has to say about ideas that relate to a wider spiritual condition than Teufelsdröckh's alone. Our minds are, of course, ripe for this process, since in Book First and occasionally in Book Second we have been told Teufelsdröckh's developing ideas have broad consequences. Our attention has been focused more sharply, however, in the early stages of Book Second on particulars of Teufelsdröckh's life, his childhood, his schooling. Still, as we have seen, in the conventionality of his love affair, the reader must feel he is being informed not just about the hero but about the reader's whole generation and naturally about himself. Carlyle now points to the generalized nature of his subject, the spiritual progress of modern man, by divorcing Teufelsdröckh's experience even further from the kinds of normal experience that take place in a concrete setting outside the mind.

The spiritualized hero, "vibrating everywhere between the highest and the lowest levels, comes into contact with public History itself" (p. 153). He encounters the Sultan of Turkey and Napoleon, pilgrims "to great Men, to great Cities, to great Events: but found there no healing" (p. 154). Here Carlyle uses the Editor to keep the solution to Teufelsdröckh's difficulties before us, to increase our impatience for him to find it, and, of course, to increase our conviction that this is the necessary conclusion. The Editor explains, "Thou foolish Teufelsdröckh! . . . Hadst thou not Greek enough to understand thus much: *The end of Man is an Action, and not a Thought*, though it were the noblest?" (p. 155, n).

No meaningful action falls in Teufelsdröckh's way, and he wanders on, losing his faith as he goes: " 'Doubt had darkened into Unbelief,' says he; 'shade after shade goes grimly over your soul, till you have the fixed, starless, Tartarean black' " (p. 159). He questions the existence of God, but while he stands, "as so many have done, shouting question after question into the Sibyl-Cave of Destiny" (p. 161), the "Infinite nature of Duty" remains "dimly present" to him.

As he moves toward the "Everlasting No," Teufelsdröckh's "Baphometic Fire-baptism," Carlyle opens up
Teufelsdröckh's mind and forces the reader to participate
in the solution of Teufelsdröckh's spiritual difficulties.
Carlyle represents with burning intensity the processes
of insight that lead eventually through the "Everlasting
Yea." In general, Teufelsdröckh the older man recreates
an internal dialogue, asking the rhetorical questions he
had posed in that past state and putting forth the successive insights he came to, evaluating them by the standards of the mature Clothes Philosophy. For example,
when the young Teufelsdröckh feels his "Workings
amounted as yet simply to—Nothing," the older Teufelsdröckh comments, "How then could I believe in my
Strength, when there was as yet no mirror to see it in?
Ever did this agitating, yet, as I now perceive, quite frivolous question, remain to me insoluble: Hast thou a certain
Faculty, a certain Worth, such even as the most have not;
or art thou the completest Dullard of these modern
times? Alas, the fearful Unbelief is unbelief in yourself;
and how could I believe?" (p. 163). The central question
is an important one and difficult to confront without reflection on one's own capacities, yet the mature Teufelsdröckh knows it is "quite frivolous." The sureness of his
voice makes us trust him implicitly. He holds the answer
for which we hope, both for Teufelsdröckh and for
ourselves.

Teufelsdröckh reaches his lowest point in contemplat-
ing death. The universe itself seems dead, but a vague
light keeps him from suicide: "From Suicide a certain
aftershine (*Nachschein*) of Christianity withheld me:
perhaps also a certain indolence of character; for, was

not that a remedy I had at any time within reach?" (p. 165). His state of mind is not indolent, however. Teufelsdröckh does not fear death in this transitional state, but he suffers a horrible, undefined anxiety: "And yet, strangely enough, I lived in a continual, indefinite, pining fear; tremulous, pusillanimous, apprehensive of I knew not what; it seemed as if all things in the Heavens above and the Earth beneath would hurt me; as if the Heavens and the Earth were but boundless jaws of a devouring monster, wherein I, palpitating, waited to be devoured" (p. 166). Teufelsdröckh's response to the Everlasting No expels this anxiety and brings partial relief to Teufelsdröckh and to the reader. In the Rue Saint-Thomas de l'Enfer he defies death and Tophet:

All at once, there rose a Thought in me, and I asked myself: "What *art* thou afraid of? Wherefore, like a coward, dost thou forever pip and whimper, and go cowering and trembling? Despicable biped! what is the sum-total of the worst that lies before thee? Death? Well, Death; and say the pangs of Tophet too, and all that the Devil and Man may, will or can do against thee! Hast thou not a heart; canst thou not suffer whatsoever it be; and, as a Child of Freedom, though outcast, trample Tophet itself under thy feet, while it consumes thee? Let it come, then; I will meet it and defy it!" And as I so thought, there rushed like a stream of fire over my whole soul; and I shook base Fear away from me forever. I was strong, of unknown strength; a spirit, almost a god.

[p. 167]

In passages like this Carlyle fuses all the reader's interests. Teufelsdröckh's speech is both *lexis* and *praxis*. By creating an internal exhortation, Carlyle connotes the intense, troubled state of Teufelsdröckh, which we, of course, wish to see resolved. He gives Teufelsdröckh's words the force and authority of the experience that is implicit in them. Furthermore, he creates a character fully able to articulate what he learns from that experience, able to speak the truth. The truth he speaks is a step toward the solution of the problem posed by *Sartor*, how to find certainty and engage in meaningful action in the modern world. Because we have become engaged in this problem and involved in its solution, the exhortation works directly on us. By repeating its words in our minds we are very much subjected to its force.

The experience described here is closed in mystical terms. Teufelsdröckh feels "a stream of fire" and becomes strong. But this feeling is a result of the crucial intuition quickened by different, largely implicit experience, not a cause. What happens at the core of the crucial mental experience is "a Thought." This thought does not come by careful philosophical deduction, nor does it come in an unprovoked flash from heaven. It comes out of a perfectly recognizable form of insight or intuition, one in which the reader has become involved.[18] The

[18] See Harrold's "The Mystical Element in Carlyle (1827–34)," *MP*, 39 (1932), 459–75. Harrold restricts himself to pointing out parallels between Carlyle and mystics, though he comes closer to calling Carlyle a mystic in "Carlyle and the Mystical Tradition," *The Catholic World*, 142 (1936), 45–49. G. B. Tennyson, who wishes Carlyle to be a Christian so he cannot be called a fascist, is willing to call Carlyle a mystic (*Sartor Called Resartus*, pp. 313–28). The question of Carlyle's relationship to Christianity and Christian revelation is thorny. Basil Willey goes along with Froude in saying that Carlyle is an "escaped Puritan" retaining certain intuitions from his Calvinist background. See his essay "Thomas Carlyle," in *Nineteenth Century Studies: Coleridge to Matthew Arnold* (New York: Columbia Univ. Press, 1949), 105–25. In *Carlyle and German Thought, 1819–1834*, Yale Studies in English, 82

reader can understand the necessity of this act of defiance, is well prepared for it, and accepts it with relief, for Teufelsdröckh and for himself, particularly if he has felt some of Teufelsdröckh's own uncertainty in the face of the Everlasting No.

To affirm our understanding of the ideas put forth and to assure our not reading psychological meaning beyond the truth Teufelsdröckh stated, Carlyle has the Editor rehearse the lesson learned. He also assures us that this is one positive step that is by no means the last. Teufelsdröckh still feels unrest but not hopeless unrest: "For the fire-baptised soul, long so scathed and thunder-riven, here feels its own Freedom, which feeling is its Bapho-

(New Haven: Yale Univ. Press, 1934), Harrold argues that Carlyle found in the Germans a theoretical basis for a moral conscience and religious convictions he had before he went to them, not a source of new ideas. In "The Nature of Carlyle's Calvinism," *SP*, 33 (1936), 475–86, Harrold again is satisfied to point out parallels between Calvinism and Carlyle's thought. René Wellek in *Immanuel Kant in England, 1793–1838* (Princeton: Princeton Univ. Press, 1931) also sees Carlyle as essentially a Christian, a Puritan, a mystic who found in the Germans only new formulas for old patterns of thought (see esp. p. 201). But more recently, in "Thomas Carlyle," in *The Age of Transition*, Vol. III of *A History of Modern Criticism, 1750–1950* (New Haven: Yale Univ. Press, 1965), he calls Carlyle a Puritan making a new religion "which cannot be described as Christianity" (p. 102). As is so often the case with attempts to explain the sources of Carlyle's ideas, one is left with a deeper sense of his originality. See also Hill Shine, *Carlyle's Fusion of Poetry, History, and Religion by 1834* (Chapel Hill: Univ. of North Carolina Press, 1937). In the matter of Carlyle's view of inspiration, he apparently did not see the possibility of inspiration from outside: "Is not every Thought properly an Inspiration? Or how is one thing more *inspired* than another? Much is in this" (*TN*, p. 166). This notion is a justification for clothing Teufelsdröckh's and all men's thought in the traditional language of inspiration.

metic Baptism: the citadel of its whole kingdom it has thus gained by assault, and will keep inexpugnable; outwards from which the remaining dominions, not indeed without hard battling, will doubtless by degrees be conquered and pacificated" (p. 169). The generalized terms he uses are an important affirmation of the inclusive significance of the intuition recorded. The Editor speaks of "the" soul, not Teufelsdröckh's exclusively, but any soul moving toward a healthful attitude toward the world and meaningful action. Carlyle's method is risky because he must make the reader feel he is pointing to a real truth about the world. If he had chosen to represent a single spiritual progress, we might accept a few oddities as due to the present character's particular situation and personality. By choosing to talk about the spiritual progress of a generation, Carlyle must perform the more difficult task of convincing us he is right in the general where we might accept the particular without question.

Teufelsdröckh's and our education continues. The "Centre of Indifference" begins in a calm.[19] Carlyle uses the Editor to focus attention back on Teufelsdröckh as a discrete individual and not on his mind in turmoil over eternal questions. The perspective given is relaxing and removes the reader from the stress of crucial insights. As a sign of the new stability at the center of Teufelsdröckh's being, the Editor quotes fragments that "exhibit him in a much more natural state" (p. 170). What the Editor quotes, however, does more than show Teufels-

[19] George Levine has noticed patterns of emotion in the book, moving from a neutral point to "a climax of faith and affirmation" ("*Sartor Resartus* and the Balance of Fiction," p. 66). He seems to be describing the shifts in rhetorical intensity that Carlyle works.

dröckh's improving health. The passages are reflections on elements of the Clothes Philosophy, including the familiar passage on war, which become bits of persuasion themselves. These are internalized exhortations, just as the crucial passages of the "Everlasting No" are internalized. And they appear to show how Teufelsdröckh can "at least in lucid intervals look away from his own sorrows, over the many-coloured world, and pertinently enough note what is passing there" (p. 175). But sympathy for Teufelsdröckh at this point only reinforces what we know intuitively, that these passages fill out the mature Clothes Philosophy, with which we have become increasingly familiar. We know the ideas of the implied orator so well that we are attentive to these passages not only as the Editor presents them, as evidence of Teufelsdröckh's improving health, but also as further exhortation to belief in the Clothes Philosophy.

In "The Centre of Indifference" Teufelsdröckh's experience is broadened even more than it has been, but in a rather mechanical way. The Editor explains that with even a little self-control "what an incredible knowledge of our Planet, and its Inhabitants and their Works, that is to say, of all knowable things, might not Teufelsdröckh acquire!" (p. 176). We learn summarily that he has "read in most Public Libraries," seen most "great Scenes," and met most "great Men" (pp. 176–78). This obvious attempt to give Teufelsdröckh's voice the authority of universal knowledge is not convincing, nor is it important next to the authority of Teufelsdröckh's rhetoric when he speaks out of intense spiritual and intellectual experience, as in the "Everlasting No." Carlyle seems to sense this, and after the democratic nonsense about horse-pistols in the Arctic, the Editor calls the reader back to the "inner man of Teufelsdröckh" and to the kinds of experience that really give him authority. Teufelsdröckh now sees the need for useful action but not the way to take it: "Thou art Nothing, Nobody: true; but who, then, is Something, Somebody? For thee the Family of Man has no use; it rejects thee; thou art wholly as a dissevered limb: so be it; perhaps it is better so!" (p. 182). Teufelsdröckh is now prepared for the Everlasting Yea.

"The Everlasting Yea," the climactic chapter of Book Second, has a disordered appearance. It is given this appearance by the number and variety of arguments Carlyle gives in support of the Everlasting Yea. The chapter is unified by its constant effort to move the reader to act unselfishly according to his duty, to "love not Pleasure; love God" (p. 192). Carlyle, like any good rhetorician, uses all available grounds for exhortation to move the reader.[20] He uses the grounds of mathematical analogy: "The fraction of Life can be increased in value not so much by increasing your Numerator as by lessening your Denominator" (p. 191); the present condition of men: "Will the whole Finance Ministers and Upholsterers and Confectioners of modern Europe undertake, in joint-stock company, to make one Shoe-black HAPPY?" (p. 190); the grounds of recent history: "Close thy *Byron*,

---

[20] Kenneth Burke in *A Rhetoric of Motives*, bound with *A Grammar of Motives*, Meridian Books (1950; rpt. Cleveland: World Publishing Co., 1962), remarks that "it seems to be a fact, that the more urgent the oratory, the greater the profusion and vitality of the formal devices" (p. 581). So here with the grounds for exhortation. *A Rhetoric of Motives* is cited hereafter as *Rhetoric*.

open thy *Goethe*" (p. 192); of the heart: "Feel it in thy heart, and then say whether it is of God! This is Belief; all else is Opinion" (p. 193); the grounds of experience: "Inasmuch as all Speculation is by nature endless, formless, a vortex amid vortices: only by a felt indubitable certainty of Experience does it find any centre to revolve round, and so fashion itself into a system" (p. 196); of the clothes metaphor: "Or what is Nature? Ha! why do I not name thee GOD? Art not thou the 'Living Garment of God'?" (p. 188). This flurry of persuasion is difficult to follow and may not always be apprehended easily, but its rapidity and intensity alone make objection to however much is apprehended difficult if not impossible.[21]

[21] John Holloway in *The Victorian Sage* suggests a way of dealing with the complex problem of whether or not Carlyle's method here is dishonest. Discussing Carlyle's use of paradox, he argues that "a discussion may consist of what might be called 'nodal' propositions, with a far from immediately plain sense, but introduced, familiarized, made easier for the reader to grasp, by a variety of techniques that would indeed be sophistical, if their interpretation could be nothing but logical; but not otherwise" (p. 51). He suggests a criterion for distinguishing between sophistical and legitimate uses of emotive language which differs, appropriately, and apparently unknowingly, from the traditional view that both must be tested by logic, as Holloway himself appears to suggest in the passage just quoted. He argues that "language, even when it fails to state or describe, has a legitimate emotive power if it operates not independently, in a beautiful though empty mist, but by re-directing our attention to objects, concentrating it upon them, and thereby making us notice aspects of them that previously we had overlooked." With sophistical or illegitimate uses of emotive language, "when we turn from the language to the things of which it is alleged to speak, experience cancels our incipient emotions, and prompts us to discard a tissue of sophistical nonsense." We recognize legitimate uses of such language when "experience reinforces and completes what language began" (p. 52). Experience, not logic, becomes the test of statements. This is particularly ap-

These exhortations are delivered in the language and
atmosphere of revelation. We are made to feel that the
central attitudes proffered are the fruit of an intense
spiritual experience. Indeed, the reader may come away
from this chapter with the sense that inspiration is the
primary authority for Teufelsdröckh's message, may feel
perhaps that he has himself glimpsed the mysterious and
divine truth, though he has, of course, been subjected to
rhetorical arguments. Carlyle uses the image he has built
of Teufelsdröckh as visionary to reinforce conclusions
that are the result of a long series of reflections. Teufelsdröckh and the reader do not *see* the necessity of dutiful
action in an unanticipated flash of light. Our shared joy
at the conclusion is not wholly spontaneous but is mixed
with relief that the necessary, implicit conclusion has
been reached.

It might be argued that in "The Everlasting Yea" Carlyle merely represents what goes on in Teufelsdröckh's
mind at a crucial stage in his development, as he has done
before. After all, recreating the process of thought is a

---

propriate in the case of *Sartor*, since the objects to which attention
is called are ourselves and our world. Carlyle's propositions must
satisfy the most immediate and demanding judgment. The reader's
logical faculties may slip, but his sense of experience is unlikely
to, especially since Carlyle has been continuously drawing the
reader through the kind of experience he appeals to here. Still, in
"The Everlasting Yea" Carlyle's propositions seem more than
"nodal" and approach argument. They are sufficiently developed
that they may be worked through and found substantial, if not
purely logical. Though they are sometimes difficult and are delivered in the language and atmosphere of revelation, the reader
has more grounds for his experience to evaluate them than that of
"things" alone.

natural way of making that experience intelligible. John Stuart Mill, for example, uses it in his *Autobiography* to describe his mental crisis:

Those only are happy (I thought) who have their minds fixed on some object other than their own happiness; on the happiness of others, on the improvement of mankind, even on some art or pursuit, followed not as a means, but as itself an ideal end. Aiming thus at something else, they find happiness by the way. The enjoyments of life (such was now my theory) are sufficient to make it a pleasant thing, when they are taken *en passant*, without being made a principal object. Once make them so, and they are immediately felt to be insufficient. They will not bear a scrutinizing examination. Ask yourself whether you are happy, and you cease to be so. The only chance is to treat, not happiness, but some end external to it, as the purpose of life. Let your self-consciousness, your scrutiny, your self-interrogation, exhaust themselves on that; and if otherwise fortunately circumstanced you will inhale happiness with the air you breathe, without dwelling on it or thinking about it, without either forestalling it in imagination, or putting it to flight by fatal questioning. This theory now became the basis of my philosophy of life. And I still hold to it as the best theory for all those who have but a moderate degree of sensibility and of capacity for enjoyment, that is, for the great majority of mankind.[22]

This mode of expression is very persuasive and approaches conventional rhetoric. Mill heightens its effectiveness by stating modestly what he feels to be the universal implications of his ideas. But the passage remains subordinate to Mill's purpose of making his intellectual

[22] *Autobiography*, Library of Liberal Arts (Indianapolis: Liberal Arts Press, 1957), p. 92. Mill asserts that he had not at the time heard of "the anti-self-consciousness theory of Carlyle."

development intelligible and justifiable. He wants us to understand the choices he made and to feel they were the proper ones. If, on the other hand, he proceeded to offer a variety of arguments on a variety of grounds for unselfish activity, we would begin to suspect his intentions, to accuse him of proselytizing.

In "The Everlasting Yea" Carlyle goes beyond simple representation of a process of thought. He achieves a powerful form of exhortation, and the reader's attention is broadened fully from Teufelsdröckh's spiritual development to include his own.[23] When, for example, Teufelsdröckh closes the chapter with an exhortation to himself to work, we are aware that his words reflect a change in himself, but we feel even more fully their effect on us: "I too could now say to myself: Be no longer a Chaos, but a World, or even Worldkin. Produce! Produce! Were it but the pitifullest infinitesimal fraction of a Product, produce it, in God's name! 'Tis the utmost thou hast in thee: Out with it, then. Up, up! Whatsoever thy hand findeth to do, do it with thy whole might. Work while it is called Today; for the Night cometh, wherein no man can work"

---

[23] David Daiches in *Carlyle and the Victorian Dilemma*, Thomas Green Lectures, No. 4 (Edinburgh: Carlyle Society, 1963), suggests that in passing from the Everlasting No to the Everlasting Yea, Carlyle substitutes rhetoric for logic. Carlyle would appear, then, merely a weaker thinker than Mill. But Carlyle does not employ all this rhetoric to convince himself, but to convince the reader. Of course, the rhetoric covers defects in logic, but it forces movement of the imagination, the faculty on which Carlyle's thought and persuasion depends. One can object to the substitution of the rhetoric of the imagination and of intuitive experience for logical argument, but one must recognize that he is objecting to a whole mode of thought and conduct, not simply to a momentary deficiency in persuasion.

(p. 197). Our sense that we are being addressed directly is buttressed by Carlyle's continuous generalizing of the implications of Teufelsdröckh's insights. Even Teufelsdröckh's introduction to this exhortation, "I *too* could now say," suggests the communal significance of what he has learned. Alvan S. Ryan has suggested that Teufelsdröckh cannot address the reader directly because the Editor is constantly interposed between Teufelsdröckh and the reader.[24] But though some of the trappings of the narrative support this point of view, in passages like the above what Teufelsdröckh says and even his manner is so consistent with the essence of what has been said throughout the book, with the implied orator's words, that the mind does not hesitate over the details of narrative. We know whom Carlyle is talking to. We feel the force of his imperatives directly.

The implications of Teufelsdröckh's conversion are brought home to us in other ways. As Harrold points out in his note to the passage quoted above, Carlyle uses phrasing that echoes the Bible. It is plain that this phrasing is not intended simply to reveal the particular way in which Teufelsdröckh thinks or addresses himself, but to stir a deep response in the reader, to make him feel the truths presented have ancient and profound authority and universal implications.[25] These Biblical echoes are consistent with the rest of Carlyle's presentation of Teufelsdröckh's experience. His passage out of the Centre of

[24] "The Attitude Toward the Reader in Carlyle's *Sartor Resartus*," *VN*, No. 23 (spring 1963), 15–16.

[25] See Holloway, *The Victorian Sage*, pp. 24–26, for an example, though an overstated one, of Carlyle's use of Biblical echoes. Like Sir Thomas Browne's, Carlyle's general allusiveness implies that all authorities speak the same universal truth.

Indifference is presented as a revelation in familiar terms:
"Here, then, as I lay in that CENTRE OF INDIFFERENCE; cast,
doubtless by benignant upper Influence, into a healing
sleep, the heavy dreams rolled gradually away, and I
awoke to a New Heaven and a new Earth."[26] Our desire
to know what Teufelsdröckh learned is heightened by
such language, but we can see that the mental experience represented as producing the insights is not purely
revelation.

Carlyle undoubtedly emphasizes the inspired quality
of Teufelsdröckh's experience partly in response to what
he feels are the rational tendencies of the age.[27] He
wishes to force the reader to recognize the validity of
and to engage in processes of thought that are not purely
rational, that engage more elements of experience than
reason. Revelation or inspiration is the farthest extreme
from rationalism, and Carlyle uses that extreme to form
what is actually a compromise with rationalism. He gives
to a process of intuition, of feeling, of reflection quickened by experience the appearance of inspiration to hold
at bay those who abuse reason by disembodying it from
human concerns. All of this becomes explicit in his attack on Voltaire in "The Everlasting Yea." The eigh-
teenth century has done its work of destruction, as its
reasoning descendants, the Benthamites, continue theirs;
and it cannot aid in building, in embodying "the divine

[26] Harrold directs us to Revelation, 21:1 (p. 186n).

[27] See esp. Leonard W. Deen, "Irrational Form in *Sartor Resartus*" and Olle Holmberg, "David Hume in Carlyle's *Sartor Resartus*," *Arsberättelse*, 1933–1934 (Kungl. Humanistika Vetenskapssamsundet i Lund), pp. 99–109. Holmberg argues that Hume is
present in *Sartor* as an invisible opponent who must often be met
before Carlyle can establish his own point of view.

Spirit of that Religion in a new Mythus, in a new vehicle and vesture." It is dismissed: "Take our thanks, then, and—thyself away." The revolution will not be one of reason: "Meanwhile what are antiquated Mythuses to me? Or is the God present, felt in my own heart, a thing which Herr von Voltaire will dispute out of me; or into me?" (p. 194). Against dispute is ranged the heart. And the heart has plenty of rhetoric of its own.

In addition, the heart has the movement of history on its side, as will become even more obvious in Book Third. The new method of thought when put into practice has revolutionary implications. Carlyle has been careful to make the reader aware that Teufelsdröckh's life is bound to that of his generation. The general or conventional terms in which his life is presented, being lured into the false Eden of romantic love, standing among the mountains, visiting great men, speculating on universal contemporary problems, all these terms help us to make the natural deduction that the implied orator is telling us about the real world, about ourselves and our history, not about a specific fictional character. The dismissing of Voltaire is understood to be a cultural and social act, not simply a personal one.

Teufelsdröckh's life is blended with contemporary social and moral progress and, of course, with our own. We, like Teufelsdröckh, are to go about our present tasks with new hope and faith in the future. For Teufelsdröckh, it is to be the Priesthood of the Pen (p. 199). As we know, his experience has rendered him especially fit to speak, as he does in *Die Kleider*, and anywhere else he can, about the present condition of man.

The tendency of critics to see disorder in Book Second,

and in other parts of *Sartor*, is encouraged by the Editor. He calls it chaotic both before recording it and after. In "Prospective," the last chapter in Book First, he calls it "a gaseous-chaotic Appendix to that aqueous-chaotic Volume [*Die Kleider*]" (p. 79), and in "Pause," the last chapter in Book Second, he airs his suspicion that what has gone before is a mystification, that he and his readers have been able to see only vaguely what has been going on (pp. 202–06). He uses what Harrold calls "a curious figure," derived from allusions to *Paradise Lost*, of building "a firm Bridge for British travellers" over the chaos of the fragmented biography (p. 79). He picks up this figure again in "Pause," claiming the bridge is not completed, but "a few flying pontoons have perhaps been added" (p. 205). Though Sin and Death used the original bridge, this one is for plainer folk and built by patient effort, "the Diligence and feeble thinking Faculty of an English editor" (p. 80). In "*Sartor Resartus* and the Balance of Fiction," George Levine has noticed that "the very chaos out of which the Editor is attempting to bring meaning becomes in *Sartor* a symbol of one of its central ideas," the idea that the physical world is "apparent chaos which really bodies forth a single ultimate spiritual truth," a part of his larger doctrine that "all things are related" (p. 62). Discussing Carlyle's use of "fragments," G. B. Tennyson says that Carlyle wants the effect of chaos in order to "make the business of grouping and understanding them a joint endeavor that issues ultimately in understanding of their underlying unity" (*Sartor Called Resartus*, p. 227). What must be emphasized is that Carlyle creates the effect of chaos, not real chaos. Even in "The Everlasting Yea," which may appear disordered, although the reader may be puzzled by a specific argument, he has no doubts about the import of the whole. The reader is never allowed to feel lost in real chaos. He never feels that the implied orator has lost control of his arguments and his materials, just as one never feels that the implied, and sometimes more than implied, author of *Tristram Shandy* has lost control of his materials, regardless of what seems to be happening to Tristram. Disorder is not a structural principle in *Sartor*.

Disorder itself is a problematical but crucial term. In "Irrational Form in *Sartor Resartus*," Leonard W. Deen speaks of "Carlyle's use of symbolism, apparent disorder, and above all fictional 'personality' or biography as methods of correcting a rationalistic organization or interpretation of reality by an exploration and expression of the mystery and creative vitality and disorder of experience" (p. 439). Experience that can be seen to lead to growth and change is orderly. The emphasis of Teufelsdröckh's rhetorical biography is always, explicitly and metaphorically, on growth of the spirit through intuition quickened by experience. Such experience is disordered only from the point of view of pure reason. Teufelsdröckh makes the following statement about the need for action:

But indeed Conviction, were it never so excellent, is worthless till it convert itself into Conduct. Nay properly Conviction is not possible till then; inasmuch as all Speculation is by nature endless, formless, a vortex amid vortices: only by a felt indubitable certainty of Experience does it find any centre to revolve round, and so fashion itself into a system. Most true is it, as a wise man teaches us, that "Doubt of any sort cannot be removed except by Action." On which ground, too, let him who gropes painfully in darkness or uncertain light, and prays vehemently that the dawn may ripen into day, lay this other precept well to heart, which to me was of invaluable service: *"Do the Duty which lies nearest thee,"* which thou knowest to be a Duty! Thy second Duty will already have become clearer.

[pp. 195–96]

For Carlyle order comes out of speculation that is stabilized by experience, not out of the exercise of reason in isolation. This may appear irrational to some, but it is certainly intelligible, humane, and sane. *Sartor* is based on the order of intuition quickened by experience, though it is sometimes, for rhetorical reasons, given the appearance of disorder.

⟩ Carlyle's position is not rational, but at its core it is not simply antirational either. In *The Victorian Frame of Mind: 1830–1870* Walter E. Houghton points to Carlyle's typical Victorian anti-intellectualism.[28] But in *Sartor* Carlyle is more and less than an anti-intellectual. In *Sartor* the view presented of the origin of ideas is typically Romantic. Ideas are the result of experience, both internal and external, born of observation, reflection, conflicting emotions, passion, not, as Carlyle would sometimes make us feel, of divine revelation and certainly not of pure reason. But experience is an organic process that continues, while the certainty Carlyle desires is stable. In *The Poetry of Experience* Robert Langbaum remarks that Carlyle, like Goethe, forgets that experience which gives authority to ideas cannot be ar-

[28] New Haven: Yale Univ. Press, 1957, pp. 129–33. See also Houghton's "Victorian Anti-Intellectualism," *Journal of the History of Ideas*, 13 (1952), 291–313.

rested (p. 20). Yet by arresting it, Carlyle passes consciously beyond the Romantic phase and into a new one.[29] He does not "forget" to continue experience. He desires a respite in conviction from the "vortex of existence" (p. 150) and of experience he and his generation have tumbled through, and he makes his reader desire it as well, for himself, for Teufelsdröckh, and for his contemporaries. Carlyle's resolution of the problem of ever-wandering experience is sophisticated and intuitively quite satisfying. Action itself is made a means of quieting restless doubt. Action might appear to lead to more experience and possibly more confusion or only to tentative resolutions, but Carlyle clearly intends action to be external, outside the mind. Romantic adventure of the mind with all its risks comes to a natural close in Victorian reliance on dutiful action. We latter-day romantics may suspect a certain faint-heartedness in Carlyle's desire for certainty, may prefer Tennyson's Ulysses to Teufelsdröckh, but we are less likely to smile in false tolerance when Carlyle has made us feel and possibly share the potential self-consuming disorder of a mind subject to experience that does not resolve itself into any stable order. Anyone who has ever doubted his own or another's ability to order experience knows the at least temporary therapeutic value of dutiful action. Carlyle's rhetoric is based on a truth our experience confirms.

Book Second is, then, part of a persuasive essay. It has

---

[29] Cassirer points to "this emphasis on man's activity, on his practical life and practical duties as the unromantic feature in Carlyle's philosophy" (*Myth*, p. 202). The emphasis on work may help account for the book's increased popularity in the mid- and late-Victorian eras.

the specific function of confirming ideas by creating in part an experience capable of producing them. The created experience, however, is carefully restricted by a variety of commentary so that it does not usurp interest from the ideas produced but rather increases our understanding of them and willingness to act according to them. Book Second is arranged as a fictional biography that is gradually modified until it becomes a sophisticated kind of exhortation. The intuitive and experiential logic of the ideas is reiterated in the life of Teufelsdröckh, and the growth of the young man parallels the growth of ideas. The ideas themselves are given coherence and authority by their origin in experience. Book Second performs a necessary function in *Sartor*.

5: The Progress of
Sartor Resartus

From what has been said, our readers
will gather, with sufficient assurance,
that the work before us is a sort of philosophical romance, in which the author
undertakes to give, in the form of a review of a German treatise on dress, and
a notice of the life of the writer, his own
opinions upon Matter and Things in
General.

NORTH AMERICAN REVIEWER[1]

Sartor Resartus is shaped by a line of rhetorical arguments, proceeding from certain premises, the Clothes
Philosophy, and strung on a unique, fictionalized mode
of speaking. The work is coherent, a complete act of persuading. It intends to take the reader from ignorance to
understanding and belief, and it is arranged to persuade
with maximum effect. *Sartor* ends when the act of persuasion is complete.

Carlyle gives *Sartor* a semblance of narrative order.
The Editor receives Teufelsdröckh's book on Clothes,
Die Kleider, begins presenting it to the reader, breaks off
to present fragments of an autobiography of Teufelsdröckh, then returns to editing *Die Kleider* and other
documents to the end. Through the fiction of *Die Klei-*

[1] "Thomas Carlyle," *North American Review*, 41 (1835), 459.
Cited in part by Carlyle in the 1838 London edition of *Sartor* (*Sartor*, p. 320). Author identified as A. H. Everett by Dyer, p. 339.

der, Carlyle imposes some historical order on his first presentation of the Clothes Philosophy. The full title of Teufelsdröckh's volume is *"Die Kleider, ihr Werden und Wirken* (Clothes, their Origin and Influence)" (p. 8). The few chapters dealing with the "origin" of Clothes follow the subject in a loosely chronological fashion. Some of the other chapters in Books First and Third that deal apparently with sections of Teufelsdröckh's volume also purport to explore aspects of the subject of clothes, when Carlyle's actual subject is a much larger one. The narrative order is a convenience that serves Carlyle's whole persuasive intention. Harmony is easily worked between seeming to present an account of a man editing the work of a transcendental German philosopher and the act of persuading readers to believe in a transcendental philosophy.

The progress of *Sartor* is determined primarily by rhetorical considerations. Carlyle requires some space to establish his fictional devices and the unique tone of the book, but even there he works persuasively. The book progresses by statement of the Clothes Philosophy and its implications, by exhortation to believe in it, by presentation of examples and other evidence, by reiteration and restatement, by anticipation and meeting of objections, by suggestion and tentative statement, by overstatement and qualification, in short, by the careful arrangement of arguments and other rhetorical devices to lead the reader to believe in and to act on the Clothes Philosophy.

The establishment and continued use of fictional devices in *Sartor* aids Carlyle by creating an unusual, engaging, implicit mode of speaking and by allowing him great flexibility in arranging his arguments, in shifting from one subject to another and from one tone to another. As we have seen, the Editor permits a variety of rhetorical maneuvers. Through the device of the fictional volume, *Die Kleider*, Carlyle can shift subjects with apparent abruptness. One of the most important effects of the fictional devices is a kind of psychological distancing they allow to take place. They increase our willingness to accept ideas in an imaginative way,[2] at least momentarily, without subjecting them to the empirical and crudely scientific tests to which we habitually subject ideas that pretend to truth. This distancing can be manipulated and broken down. As suggested above, we are frequently aware that we are being told about the real world. In fact, the reference of *Sartor* to the actual must have been felt even more powerfully by Carlyle's contemporaries, who did not need footnotes in order to grasp specific allusions. Carlyle seems to be in control of this distancing effect, which can work both for him, by reducing the anxieties and other feelings we have about ideas that may affect our lives, and against him, by encouraging us not to take his ideas seriously. His control extends to all of his fictional devices, the Editor, Teufelsdröckh, the Hofrath, *Die Kleider*; all serve his persuasive intention. His use of fictional devices and an implicit mode of speaking is coordinated with a progressive development

[2] Cf. Norman N. Holland's discussion of Carlyle's "masking" in "Prose and Minds: A Psychoanalytic Approach to Non-Fiction," in *The Art of Victorian Prose*, ed. George Levine and William Madden (New York: Oxford Univ. Press, 1968), pp. 314–37. Holland's stimulating account of Carlyle's method and of reader responses to nonfiction is based on a different psychology from the one assumed in the present study.

of rhetorical arguments for the Clothes Philosophy. These elements determine the form of *Sartor*. Furthermore, the three books into which it is divided are necessary parts of the whole form. Each performs slightly different tasks, but all three books contribute to the progress and integrity of the whole.

These assertions demand some demonstration. In order to clarify the progress of Carlyle's rhetoric in *Sartor*, the rest of this chapter will outline the argument of Book First, suggest the necessity of Book Second, and examine the sequence of Book Third in some detail.

The purpose of Book First is to introduce most of the elements of the Clothes Philosophy and to establish Carlyle's fictionalized mode of speaking, to acquaint us with the Editor, with Teufelsdröckh, and with the implied orator who operates through them. Carlyle tends to compose in short chapters, each defining a set subject, usually named by the title, and each linked to previous and succeeding chapters by the course of his whole argument. The first four chapters, "Preliminary," "Editorial Difficulties," "Reminiscences," and "Characteristics," deal with the arrival of Teufelsdröckh's volume, the arrangements for publishing it, and the Editor's limited account of Teufelsdröckh's character. The apparent narrative here has the obvious advantage of novelty. The reader is likely to sense the strong and important arguments being made through the Editor and Teufelsdröckh. At the same time, a part of his mind is likely to respond naively to the fictions, to function like the cavemen E. M. Forster imagines hunched around a fire, wondering implacably, to the storyteller's discomfort, what will hap-

pen next.[3] No plot arises to nourish higher forms of curiosity, but the play of Carlyle's narrative is amusing.
Through the narrative Carlyle establishes important
ideas: the need to investigate man's situation with clari-
ty, the difficulties of knowing the truth with certainty in
this disordered world, the possibility of coming to know
through a "clear logically-founded Transcendentalism"
(p. 16), which Teufelsdröckh seems created to help us
achieve. The most trivial details echo with significance.
Order can be wrought even out of the littered chaos of
Teufelsdröckh's apartment by a properly determined and
silent housekeeper (pp. 24–25).

The possibility of coming to knowledge lies in the attitudes and powers attributed to Teufelsdröckh. He pos-
sesses wonder, determination, descendentalism which
sees through the shame of the present, and transcendentalism which tries to pierce through to the essential and
timeless. He has the power of "a wild Imagination
wedded to the clearest Intellect" (p. 31). These attitudes
and this power are encouraged in us, explicitly by Teufelsdröckh and implicitly by Carlyle's mode of urging
truths through a lively and disorderly narrative.

We are led to think that the ideas presented and to be
presented to us are coherent, in spite of many hints that
Die Kleider, the Clothes Philosophy, and even *Sartor* itself
are disordered. Carlyle's purpose in suggesting that the
Professor is not orderly or systematic could be simply,
as many have taken it to be, an apology for Carlyle's own
inability to control his thought and speech. It could be
intended to divert criticism of an implied orator who cannot hold his materials together. But Carlyle has another

[3] *Aspects of the Novel* (New York: Harcourt, Brace, 1927), p. 46.

purpose in insisting that there is more chaos in *Sartor* than there actually is. He makes a virtue of disorder: "It were a piece of vain flattery to pretend that this work on Clothes entirely contents us; that it is not, like all works of genius, like the very Sun, which, though the highest published creation, or work of genius, has nevertheless black spots and troubled nebulosities amid its effulgence, —a mixture of insight, inspiration, with dulness, double-vision, and even utter blindness" (p. 28). Teufelsdröckh is made to appear a rough natural genius "like the very Sun," the opposite of the dandified upper classes. He has "a strange scientific freedom; like a man unversed in the higher circles, like a man dropped thither from the Moon" (p. 29). He is "not a cultivated writer," and he speaks in tattered sentences in "a wild tone" (p. 31). "He speaks-out with a strange plainness; calls many things by their mere dictionary names" (p. 29). "In our wild Seer, shaggy, unkempt, like a Baptist living on locusts and wild honey, there is an untutored energy, a silent, as it were unconscious strength, which except in the higher walks of Literature, must be rare" (p. 30). He may show "want of intercourse with the higher classes" (p. 31), but his roughness is that of the best literature. He is made to appear more of a Biblical or Puritan figure, than one from "learned, indefatigable, deep-thinking Germany" (p. 6). He is a plain speaker.[4]

[4] Carlyle remarks in "Characteristics," written late in the fall of 1831, several months after the completion of *Sartor*, about the superiority of the "Natural over the Artificial": "Again, in the difference between Oratory and Rhetoric, as indeed everywhere in that superiority of what is called the Natural over the Artificial, we find a similar illustration. The Orator persuades and carries all with him: the one is in a state of healthy unconsciousness, as if he

Before he begins presenting the Clothes Philosophy, the Editor complains again about *Die Kleider*, that "it is true, his adherence to the mere course of Time produces, through the Narrative portions, a certain show of outward method; but of true logical method and sequence there is too little" (p. 34). The Editor's attempt to "bring what order we can out of this chaos" (p. 34) reflects Carlyle's idea that the chaos of the world actually embodies a single truth and reflects his belief that this truth is not to be perceived through ordinary logic. Furthermore, the disorder to which the Editor calls attention exists primarily in *Die Kleider*. The godlike act of leading us to perceive order in that chaos is performed for us by the arrangement of and commentary on *Die Kleider* in *Sartor*, and even the sequence of Teufelsdröckh's tome, which the Editor claims to follow, seems to make some sense. When the order of the argument in Books First and Third is perceived, Carlyle's suggestion that the presentation of the Clothes Philosophy is disordered seems extravagant and perhaps designed to throw the reader off guard, as well as to enforce certain ideas. We are never brought to feel that the implied orator has lost control of his argument, that what we are reading is genuinely disordered. Calling attention to potential disorder prepares us for the particular intensity of speech to which we are subjected, prepares us for the rhetoric of the imagination through which Carlyle speaks.

In Chapter V, "The World in Clothes," the Editor begins presenting the "Historical-Descriptive" (p. 34) part

---

'had no system'; the other, in virtue of regimen and dietetic punctuality, feels at best that 'his system is in high order' " (*Works*, 28:7).

of *Die Kleider.* The succeeding chapters follow a loose chronological order, which is frequently brushed aside, so that Carlyle can pursue his argument in the most effective way. Pretending to present a history of clothes is useful because it allows Carlyle to develop two crucial ideas, often through metaphors. The first is the idea that what we consider reality is only a creation of the senses, an unreality masking accurately or inaccurately the essential, spiritual reality beyond. The second is that history is organic, a "Tissue," which "inweaves all Being" (p. 22). By presenting some actual history of clothes, Carlyle can convince us that clothing, the outer mask of our inner selves, changes, and that past clothing is connected with present clothing.

From Chapter V through the remainder of Book First, Carlyle carefully expands our sense of what the Clothes Philosophy means. One of his central methods of persuasion here is through the expansion of metaphors and of metaphorical language. He creates an apparently fresh language, which actually bears many permanent associations, and uses it to create new perceptions. He uses the subject of clothes, for example, as an oblique way of talking about progress, about what man is, has become, and is capable of becoming. As he talks, however, he builds a vocabulary that assumes his central meanings and makes his speech more direct and less oblique.[5] His vocabulary of clothes gradually becomes a vocabulary of metaphysics, capable of including all relationships in the universe within its terms. The vocabulary of clothes becomes so generalized and allusive that it runs the risk of

[5] See Holloway's discussion of "The Growth of Metaphor" in *The Victorian Sage,* pp. 36–41.

becoming transparent and simply inconvenient. In general, however, Carlyle controls his meanings so carefully by context and syntax that what he is saying is seldom in doubt, though the implications may be accepted without proper evaluation.

Certain crucial implications remain rooted in the word "clothes," no matter how clear it is that the word is being applied to complex social relationships—as in the remark "Society is founded upon Cloth" (p. 51)—to the nature of the world as *the living visible Garment of God*" (p. 55), or to the dress men wear. Clothes are impermanent: "Thus is the law of Progress secured; and in Clothes, as in all other external things whatsoever, no fashion will continue" (p. 47). But clothes are also always present in one form or another, always necessary and always being replaced. Thus the term "clothes" has implicit in it Carlyle's major concerns, flux and permanency, or at least consistency, in that flux. Often Carlyle lapses into a more conventional vocabulary, but he returns to terms of clothing, generally because of the implications they have, which more neutral conventional terms do not have.

In his presentation of the "Historical-Descriptive" section of *Die Kleider*, Carlyle parodies, abuses, and uses the methods of the historical survey, a form of writing he had done himself. Teufelsdröckh will not write any "Cause-and-Effect Philosophy of Clothes," for "such Philosophies have always seemed to me uninstructive enough . . . naked Facts, and Deductions drawn therefrom in quite another than that omniscient style, are my humbler and proper province" (p. 36). But the fiction of the Editor allows Carlyle to telescope all these facts, to hint at their presence without detailing them and even to laugh a bit at such pedantry. Through the Editor, who is made to select from this "true concentrated and purified Learning" (p. 39), Carlyle can present what historical examples he wants and give the half-serious impression that exhaustive presentation of the evidence would yield the same conclusions.

The sequential history of clothes begun in "The World in Clothes" reemerges at the beginning of the next two chapters, "Aprons" and "Miscellaneous-Historical," but it remains indistinct. Instead of following it closely, Carlyle enforces by many available means the central idea that man has great potential power which he uses vainly. In "The World in Clothes" Carlyle has the Editor indicate the encyclopedic nature of Teufelsdröckh's learning, then has him quote reflective passages. These passages argue for man's ability to create clothing and tools which give him organization and power, which he misuses: "Clothes gave us individuality, distinctions, social polity; Clothes have made Men of us; they are threatening to make Clothes-screens of us" (p. 41). The apparent disjunctiveness of this portion of Book First disappears when the single direction of Carlyle's remarks is grasped. His desire to urge us to understand our power and how we abuse it flows over into exhortation to us to use it properly: "Cast forth thy Act, thy Word, into the ever-living, ever-working Universe" (p. 40). The natural compelling force of understanding is prodded by the authoritative imperative. In fact, in Book Second we feel that the imperatives Teufelsdröckh directs at himself, "Produce! Produce!" (p. 197), are directed just as fully at us, because we have become accustomed by then to being addressed in this way.

In addition to arousing our sense of power, Carlyle
suggests directions it might take. He takes up a special
kind of clothes in the next chapter, "Aprons." The Editor
seems not to understand why Teufelsdröckh should
mention three aprons used in defiance of monarchical
authority. Then using "aprons" as he uses "clothes," the
Professor toys with the idea of social institutions that
function like aprons. He remarks that "of all Aprons the
most puzzling to me hitherto has been the Episcopal or
Cassock," which seems to be done with its work (p. 44).
He suggests further that "the Journalists are now the
true Kings and Clergy" (p. 45). Carlyle does not press
these revolutionary doctrines very hard, as he will in
Book Third. But the implication of a need to chasten
present authority remains in the examples given of the
luxurious vanity of dresses from past ages. Lurking in
the background of these examples, as it is in the whole
discussion of clothes, is contemporary English dandyism,
an open target in the concluding chapters of Book Third.
Earlier, Carlyle alludes to the "Anglo-Dandiacal" archi-
tectural idea of clothes (p. 35). Again, he remarks, "The
first spiritual want of a barbarous man is Decoration, as
indeed we still see among the barbarous classes in civ-
ilised countries."[6] His sarcasm is plain when he remarks
that in the fifteenth century men wore "doublets of fus-
tian, under which lie multiple ruffs of cloth, pasted together with batter (*mit Teig zusammen-gekleistert*),
which create protuberance enough. Thus do the two
sexes vie with each other in the art of Decoration; and
as usual the stronger carries it" (p. 48). The absurd quotation of the pseudo-original German phrase in a parody

[6] Cf. Arnold's "Barbarians" in *Culture and Anarchy.*

of scholarship is a key to the light, tentative spirit of Book First in contrast with the more sober, direct tone of Book Third.

The implications of Book First are clear, however, and become even a bit unnerving when the section on the origin and improvement of clothes ends with an example of pure simplicity in dress. The example is not the prophet in loincloth, but the trooper of Bolivar's cavalry in his blanket, which serves as shelter and shield for battle. The militaristic, authoritarian Carlyle who appears more openly in later works is present in *Sartor.* The power men have is physical as well as spiritual. The first blast of gunpowder "drove Monk Schwartz's pestle through the ceiling." The last will "achieve the final undisputed prostration of Force under Thought, of Animal courage under Spiritual" (p. 40). At least, at this stage of his career he saw gunpowder also as an equalizing force to put down Russian smugglers and make "all men alike tall" (p. 180), and he saw warfare as a victimizing of the innocent soldiers by their leaders (p. 175).

In Chapter VIII "The World out of Clothes," Carlyle has the Editor begin to present the second part of *Die Kleider,* the "Speculative-Philosophical portion," which deals with the *"Wirken,* or Influences" of Clothes. The arguments begun in Chapter VIII continue through the next two chapters, "Adamitism" and "Pure Reason." The organization of these three chapters is complex both because of the difficulty of the arguments being made and because of the rhetorical necessity to anticipate objections and misunderstandings. Carlyle pursues the double effort of attacking vanity in order to free the reader from it and its products, and of encouraging an attitude of wonder at the universe and at the self and its powers, mixing "Descendentalism" with "Transcendentalism" (p. 65). The task is not an easy one. Vanity in man's uses of power and in his view of himself is easy to find and easy to ridicule: "shall I speak it?—the Clothes fly-off the whole dramatic corps; and Dukes, Grandees, Bishops, Generals, Anointed Presence itself, every mother's son of them, stand straddling there, not a shirt on them; and I know not whether to laugh or weep" (p. 61). Teufelsdröckh reduces man easily to, "as Swift has it, 'a forked straddling animal with bandy legs.' " But it is not easy to induce a reader, with all this evidence of man's vanity about him, to believe that man is "also a Spirit, and unutterable Mystery of Mysteries" (p. 57). Carlyle has difficulty rooting the sense of man's divine qualities in anything but abstractions: "The thing Visible, nay the thing Imagined, the thing in any way conceived as Visible, what is it but a Garment, a Clothing of the higher, celestial Invisible, 'unimaginable, formless, dark with excess of bright'?" (p. 67).[7]

The spiritual view of man can be defined partly against its strongest opposition, science and Benthamism. In doing so, Carlyle reverts to the human mind and the nature of perception, suggesting a distinction he makes more explicit in Book Third: " 'To the eye of vulgar Logic,' says he, 'what is man? An omnivorous Biped that wears Breeches. To the eye of Pure Reason what is he? A Soul, a Spirit, and divine Apparition. Round his mysterious ME, there lies, under all those wool-rags, a Garment of Flesh (or of Senses), contextured in the Loom of Heaven;

[7] Harrold says that this is a misquotation of Milton, *Paradise Lost*, III, 1. 380: "Dark with *excessive* bright" (*Sartor*, p. 67n).

whereby he is revealed to his like, and dwells with them in UNION and DIVISION; and sees and fashions for himself a Universe, with azure Starry Spaces, and long Thousands of Years' " (p. 65). Carlyle divides the mind into separate faculties, one of which has priority over the other. "Pure reason" is, as Harrold says, "A Kantian term used here in opposition to 'vulgar logic' (Kant's 'Understanding' [*Verstand*]); for Carlyle, the moral intuition of the world of eternal values" (p. 65 n).[8] Later Carlyle substitutes "Fancy" and "imagination" for "Pure reason." But he does not deny "vulgar logic." He uses, as we have seen, the view of man as "omnivorous Biped that wears Breeches" to deflate man's false sense of achievement, just as he shows himself willing in Book Third to let the Benthamites destroy old forms to allow for the construction of new.

Carlyle's use of a Kantian term and several available synonyms makes one suspect that Carlyle uses available terms to put into a modern, attractive dress ideas that are products of his own system. His doing so also suggests a world that bodies forth one truth. Carlyle comes down rather emphatically on scripture as authority: "Why multiply instances? It is written, the Heavens and the Earth shall fade away like a Vesture; which indeed they are: the Time-vesture of the Eternal" (p. 74).[9] But the tendency to move, often in parallel phrases as he does here, to terms he has made his own makes the reader feel that the ideas are the author's and original.[10]

[8] See Harrold's "Carlyle's Interpretation of Kant," *PQ*, 7 (1928), 345–57. See also René Wellek, *Immanuel Kant in England*.

[9] Harrold cites Matthew 4:4 and Psalms 102:25, 26 (p. 74 n).

[10] An early anonymous reviewer remarked: "That details may

Carlyle uses the imagination, the superior faculty, in a variety of ways, generally to oppose the limitations science appears to place on man and to liberate men, even if only for work, for dutiful action. Imagination can mean man's ability to create in his mind what scientific logic will not permit him to apprehend. Man, as Carlyle says in the passage on pure reason just quoted, "sees and fashions for himself a Universe." Yet to persuade a reader not only to do so, but also to act on what he imagines is no simple task. Daydreaming is one matter. Acting on a view that "round this mysterious ME, there lies, under all those wool-rags, a Garment of Flesh (or of Senses), contextured in the Loom of Heaven; whereby he is revealed to his like, and dwells with them in UNION and DIVISION" is different from imagining for a moment its possibility. One testimony to the reality of such belief and action upon it is, of course, the speaker's own belief, to which Carlyle can point, by means of his fictions, in two ways. Teufelsdröckh's belief is attested to by his speech, both by its meaning and its intensity. The fervor with which the meaning is stated attests to the reality of belief. Carlyle can also have the Editor point to Teufelsdröckh's belief: "Such tendency to Mysticism is everywhere traceable in this man; and indeed, to attentive readers, must have been long ago apparent. Nothing that

---

have been suggested by a continual study of Richter and Goethe we can well believe, but nothing can induce us to believe that such a book is not the genuine utterance of the self-built convictions of a thinking mind." See "Pantagruelism," *Quarterly Review*, 81 (1847), 126. The author of this review is identified as John William Donaldson in *The Wellesley Index to Victorian Periodicals, 1824–1900*, ed. Walter E. Houghton (Toronto: Toronto Univ. Press, 1966), I, 730, Item 885.

he sees but has more than a common meaning, but has two meanings" (p. 66). An obvious way to substantiate such belief is to dwell more fully on the man and the mind that originated it, that is, to incorporate his biography, as Carlyle does in Book Second.

In "Prospective," the last chapter in Book First, Carlyle suggests the condition in which a reader might find himself, disposed to believe, but arrested by fear and by a sense of isolation. In response to this condition, he insists that all things are united and that "all objects are as windows, through which the philosophic eye looks into Infinitude itself" (p. 72). The prospect of such vision is before the reader, as is the prospect of great knowledge: "Thus in this one pregnant subject of CLOTHES, rightly understood, is included all that men have thought, dreamed, done, and been: the whole External Universe and what it holds is but Clothing, and the essence of all Science lies in the PHILOSOPHY OF CLOTHES" (p. 74). The possibilities are attractive, but Carlyle does not rely at this point on further explication of and argument for his ideas. Instead, he moves, for reasons that will be discussed, to the biography of Teufelsdröckh.

Book First, then, brings the reader to a certain point. He is familiar with Carlyle's fictionalized mode of speaking. He has been urged to believe that since he has the ability to create emblems or symbols, he has the power to change them. Since all things apparently real, especially social organization, are emblems, man's power is indeed great. Man is, of course, also limited by the very symbols he creates and will only achieve his true measure if he creates symbols corresponding, at least for his moment in history, to the proper ideas beyond the actual.

To stop here would be a mistake for Carlyle and for the reader. Certain questions must come to the reader's mind: How do I know that the world is this way? If it is this way, how am I to act? How is all of this related to me and to my life? These questions may take a more detached form. The reader may wonder what this inventive, sarcastic, eccentric but serious writer ("implied orator," if one wonders in these terms) is going to do next, how he is going to continue what he has begun. In either case, the reader is unlikely to feel that he knows all he wants to know, that the act of persuasion he has submitted himself to is complete. More persuasion is necessary.

Book Second has been discussed in detail in the previous chapter, and there is no need to reiterate a description of its rhetorical structure. It is important, however, to determine its place in the work, to see both what it contributes to *Sartor* and to see how it fits into the progress of the whole work.

The necessity for Book Second arises out of Book First. Book Second serves to substantiate the Clothes Philosophy as it has been presented and to give it a more personal force. The authority for this set of ideas is in man, his mind, his imagination, his intuition quickened by experience, and it can be shared by all men. The authority is not in Teufelsdröckh's unique mind and experience, but he has led the way. Book Second makes it possible for the reader to have a similar experience in his imagination. And these ideas can attain significance only when they are believed actively.

The necessity for Book Second lies in the ideas being

urged in *Sartor*, and its peculiar structure can be accounted for only as an attempt to move the reader to
belief and action upon those ideas. Book Second is not,
as Harrold suggests, a way of breaking the monotony of
the format of Book First and Book Third (p. xxxi). Nor
is it an attempt to resolve a consistently represented conflict between the Editor and Teufelsdröckh, though the
Editor is used to heighten the reader's desire for the potential understanding Teufelsdröckh's biography may
provide. Book Second serves primarily to urge the reader
further to a new sense of himself, of his power, and of
his ability to act: "Yes here, in this poor, miserable, ham-
pered, despicable Actual, wherein thou even now stand-
est, here or nowhere is thy Ideal: work it out therefrom;
and working, believe, live, be free" (p. 196). This statement is a great deal more persuasive after the reader has
followed the argument of Book Second than it could be
made to be in Book First. In Book First the Editor remarks, "Would to Heaven those same Biographical
Documents were come! For it seems as if the demonstration lay much in the Author's individuality; as if it were
not Argument that had taught him, but Experience" (p.
52). Argument is primarily what is available in Book
First, and experience there can only be intuited from quite
abstract language. Teufelsdröckh says, for example, about
man: "He feels; power has been given him to know, to
believe; nay does not the spirit of Love, free in its celestial primeval brightness, even here, though but for moments, look through?" (p. 66). The assertion and question remain abstract. In Book Second Carlyle gains a
much greater ability to define precise feelings, to make
Teufelsdröckh speak out of a clearly defined experience,

and to create in the reader the kind of experience that produces and substantiates the Clothes Philosophy.

The progress of Book Second, as it has been outlined in the previous chapter, is determined superficially by the conventions of biography. It begins with Teufelsdröckh's genesis and ends with his decision, as a young man, to go into the world and work. The progress of the chapter is governed more importantly by Carlyle's desire to motivate the reader both to overcome fear and indifference and to be willing to act. This persuasive intention is carried out through a variety of rhetorical means, as we have seen, narrative which becomes generalized to include both a whole generation of men and the reader, comments on the autobiographical passages which become exhortations, incidents in the biography which become examples of large truths. In general terms, Carlyle leads the reader through a series of psychological stages or states of belief, analogous to Teufelsdröckh's, making him aware that there is a secure end to them and giving him continuous hints of the nature of this end. Through the Editor, Carlyle characterizes the states through which Teufelsdröckh passes as "Growth, Entanglement, Unbelief, and almost Reprobation, into a certain clearer state of what he himself seems to consider as Conversion" (p. 198). The last state is that of the Everlasting Yea, a state of acceptance of the world and one's place in it, of a willingness to love God, not pleasure, and to work for a better society, based on true religion: "Wilt thou help us to embody the divine Spirit of that Religion in a new Mythus, in a new vehicle and vesture, that our Souls, otherwise too like perishing may live?" (p. 194).

Carlyle's work is not done yet. The state to which he has tried to lead his reader is antagonistic to many contemporary modes of perception and behavior. It is antagonistic to the pursuit of property, as Carlyle reminds us in an ironic passage in the last chapter of Book Second, "Pause." Book Second may move the reader to the Everlasting Yea, but Carlyle needs Book Third to confirm him in that state, to overcome antagonistic tendencies— such as a desire to pursue property—to direct his willingness to act, and to reassure him that his actions will have consequences for himself and for the community in the future. Like Book First, Book Second is a necessary part, but not a conclusion.

Book Third channels and expands the sense of purpose instilled by Book Second and broadens many of the ideas stated briefly and tentatively in Book First. Carlyle urges the reader to action, or to an attitude,[11] to remake society and its institutions. This reforming action is justified by the whole Clothes Philosophy, the implications of which Carlyle outlines carefully. Furthermore, Book Third is designed to persuade the reader of the necessity of furthering social change, in such a way that the reader's optimism about the future will be increased, that he will have no reason for alarm at the prospect of change. Partly because of Carlyle's practice of composing chapters dealing with distinct subjects, the sequence and integration of the chapters in Book Third has not been ob-

[11] In *Rhetoric* Kenneth Burke suggests speaking of persuasion " 'to attitude,' rather than persuasion to out-and-out action. Persuasion involves choice, will; it is directed to a man only insofar as he is *free*" (p. 574).

vious to some readers of *Sartor*. As is true throughout *Sartor*, many ideas are restated,[12] but there is progress in the rhetorical statement and development of the ideas. Carlyle leads the reader, with care for his fears and hesitations, to new understanding, new hope, and new motivation.

Briefly, in Chapter I of Book Third, "Incident in Modern History," Carlyle presents a historical example of meaningful action by an individual in an apparently powerless station, whose efforts have significant social repercussions. In the next three chapters, "Church-Clothes," "Symbols," and "Helotage," he argues that religion is the basis, the essential tissue, of society and that at present religion and, consequently, society are lifeless. He explains that social institutions, particularly religious ones, are symbols of something real and ideal and must, as time wears them away, be modified to embody better what lies behind them. Symbols must be reexamined and given new form and new life because men unite around them, especially around religious symbols. As old institutions are modified or abandoned for new ones and as men are reunited, all men must be valued, although some will be valued less than they

[12] In "*Sartor Resartus* and the Balance of Fiction" George Levine suggests, by analogy with *Past and Present*, that much of the material in Book First and Book Third is interchangeable and that Carlyle's whole method is essentially static, that the structure of the book is "a series of elaborate variations on a central position" (pp. 63–66). The work is not static, however, in its effect. The materials are constant in the sense that the ideas, as materials, are constant, but their particular persuasive statement and the rhetorical arguments given vary according to the context, so that actual passages could not be interchanged without destroying the rhetorical effect of the whole.

valued themselves before this leveling of society. In the fifth chapter, "The Phoenix," Carlyle argues that society is dying, but that a new one is being created in the midst of the destruction of the old. Carlyle then argues in "Old Clothes" for an attitude of reverence for the past and the future, for old symbols and new, for the spectacle of progressive change. The future, he says in "Organic Filaments," is at work in the present, and he gives examples of filaments working to replace the old religious tissue of society. In "Natural Supernaturalism," he indicates that the new society will depend on a hierarchy of worth which all will honor naturally, and that even within such a hierarchy all men will remain one. Further, men have the spiritual power to effect change, to aid in the realization of the Divine Idea of the world.

Carlyle then summarizes, in Chapter IX, "Circumspective," what he has said and then presents, for those who want something useful, two practical deductions from the Clothes Philosophy. The first of these, in "The Dandiacal Body," points to the distance between the rich and the poor in England as a warning of the possibility of revolution if proper action, according to the Clothes Philosophy, is not taken. The second, in "Tailors," does good-natured honor to tailors and by implication to all who remake the world. The Editor then bids the readers "Farewell," anticipating the antagonism that met the book as it appeared in *Fraser's*.

The arrangement of these chapters and of the materials in them, as is true throughout *Sartor*, is not determined simply by the logic (if that term may be used) of the ideas just outlined. It is determined by rhetorical considerations, by the desire to state ideas in the most persuasive

manner. Book Third creates attitudes toward the present
and the future that will be accompanied by strong feelings, and Carlyle works to contain and direct them. The
rhetorical progress of Book Third can be seen best by
treating the chapters in sequence in some detail.

In the first chapter of Book Third, "Incident of Modern
History," Carlyle uses a historical example to persuade
us that the lowliest individual action may have great
consequences—the destruction of old and the construction of new social forms. This actual example of the power
of individual effort gives point to the imperative to produce at the end of Book Second. The fictionalized example
of Teufelsdröckh, arrived at preparedness to work, is
succeeded by the historical example of George Fox, the
Quaker, who worked to good end. The life of George
Fox reiterates the pattern and purpose of Teufelsdröckh's:
"Mountains of encumbrance, higher than Aetna, had
been heaped over that Spirit: but it was a Spirit, and
would not lie buried there. Through long days and nights
of silent agony, it struggled and wrestled, with a man's
force, to be free; how its prison-mountains heaved and
swayed tumultously, as the giant spirit shook them to
this hand and that, and emerged into the light of Heaven!
That Leicester shoe-shop, had men known it, was a
holier place than any Vatican or Loretto-shrine" (p. 210).
His action is both destructive and constructive: "Stitch
away, thou noble Fox: every prick of that little instru-
ment is pricking into the heart of Slavery, and World-
worship, and the Mammon-god" (p. 211). His stitching
epitomizes the action or attitude Carlyle urges us to
take. The Editor interprets this "Incident in Modern History" as a piece of persuasion designed to make the

reader desire a leveling of society and adds to its persuasiveness by deriding ironically men's resistance to moral change: "Does Teufelsdröckh anticipate that, in this age of refinement, any considerable class of the community, by way of testifying against the 'Mammon-god,' and escaping from what he calls 'Vanity's Workhouse and Ragfair,' where doubtless some of them are toiled and whipped and hood-winked sufficiently,—will sheathe themselves in close-fitting cases of Leather? The idea is ridiculous in the extreme" (p. 212). The Editor speaks naturally in terms of the Clothes Philosophy, treating social change as analogous to change in clothing. His apparent disagreement turns into abuse of those who will hesitate to follow. Carlyle works on us in every imaginable way.

The next chapter, "Church-Clothes," converts this analogy between clothing and social institutions into an identity. The two sides of the analogy become interchangeable. It becomes increasingly difficult to see what is being compared to what, clothes to institutions or institutions to clothes. Our frame of reference (the "things" John Holloway feels ground in experience our response to propositions) [13] becomes more and more unstable. Carlyle moves us out of a world in which clothing may be a metaphor into one in which it is an active symbol embodying a divine principle. Church-Clothes become a highly abstract symbol:

By Church-Clothes, it need not be premised that I mean infinitely more than Cassocks and Surplices; and do not at all mean the mere haberdasher Sunday Clothes that men go to Church in. Far from it! Church-Clothes, are, in our vocabu-

[13] See chapter 4 above, note 21.

lary, the Forms, the *Vestures*, under which men have at various periods embodied and represented for themselves the Religious Principle; that is to say, invested the Divine Idea of the World with a sensible and practically active Body, so that it might dwell among them as a living and life-giving WORD.

[pp. 213–14]

Since the Church-Clothes invest *the* "Divine Idea of the World," they are crucial to a true society, assuming, that is, that the divine is intrinsically compelling. Thus Church-Clothes come to signify the whole social embodiment of the Divine Idea. The term becomes so abstract that the church and its usual attendant symbols require special designation as a subcategory, "your Church proper, and the Church-Clothes specially recognized as Church-Clothes" (p. 215).

This process of abstraction is begun tentatively in Book First, where the idea of Clothes is explored rather adventurously as a metaphor: "For matter, were it never so despicable, is Spirit, the manifestation of Spirit: were it never so honourable, can it be more? The thing Visible, nay the thing Imagined, the thing in any way conceived as Visible, what is it but a Garment, a Clothing of the higher, celestial Invisible, 'unimaginable, formless, dark with excess of bright'?" (pp. 66–67). In Book First the identity of spirit and matter is stated tentatively, speculatively, and the substitution of "Clothing" for "matter" is suggested. The substitution is completed in "Church-Clothes," but not simply to convince us the world is symbolic in terms conveniently consistent with the conceit of clothes. It is effected to impose on our notion of a symbolic world the judgment implicit in the idea of clothes.

If social institutions are clothes, they will wear out, fit badly or well, need adjustment, and can be changed at will. The power the individual and his will obtain in this world of clothes is substantial.[14]

In the following chapter, "Symbols," Carlyle moves to the more neutral term "symbol" to illuminate the process he has been engaged in. But Carlyle keeps hold on the evaluative term "clothes." Teufelsdröckh remarks, for example, that "Symbols, like all terrestrial Garments, wax old" (p. 224). When the Editor summarizes our mutual progress in "Circumspective," he says, "Nay further, art not thou too perhaps by this time made aware that all Symbols are properly Clothes; that all Forms whereby Spirit manifests itself to sense, whether outwardly or in the imagination are Clothes" (p. 270). The evaluative term ultimately encompasses the neutral one. It is also important to note that symbols may be apprehended by sense, "outwardly," or in "the imagination," as the Editor remarks here and in the quotation above from Book First. Part of the power Carlyle attributes to men is their power to manipulate and perhaps to create symbols in the imagination. This power is important, as we shall see, in overcoming what manifests itself to sense; and it makes will or desire, not ability, the necessary element in effecting change. In such a scheme persuasion becomes crucial.

In "Symbols" Carlyle's argument is a bit difficult to follow. He begins by explaining the importance of imagination or fantasy: "Fantasy being the organ of the Godlike . . . Man thereby, though based, to all seeming, on the small Visible, does nevertheless extend down into

[14] Cf. Kenneth Burke's discussion of "Old Clothes" in *Rhetoric*, pp. 642–47.

the infinite deeps of the Invisible, of which Invisible, indeed, his Life is properly the bodying forth" (pp. 217–
18).[15] He then speaks of silence and secrecy, making them
both moral and intellectual virtues on several authorities.
The relation of silence to symbols and imagination is not
immediately clear, but Carlyle uses this moral attitude
toward silence in this rhetorical context to define an attitude toward symbols, which have the virtue, like silence, of concealment combined with a further virtue,
revelation: "In a Symbol there is concealment and yet
revelation: here therefore, by Silence and by Speech
acting together, comes a double significance" (p. 219).
Symbols reveal the infinite, which is itself compelling: "By Symbols, accordingly, is man guided and com-
manded, made happy, made wretched. He everywhere
finds himself encompassed with Symbols, recognized as
such or not recognised: the Universe is but one vast
Symbol of God; nay if thou wilt have it, what is man
himself but a Symbol of God" (p. 220).

Carlyle then reaches out to catch up those still somewhere short of denying the Everlasting No, to whom the
universe is an indifferent and threatening machine (p.
164). The "Motive-Millwrights," Teufelsdröckh says,
have fancied that man is "a dead Iron-balance for weigh-
ing Pains and Pleasures on" and the universe a grinding
"Mechanism" (pp. 220–21). One might hesitate and ask
why this is not their right, since "the thing Imagined,

[15] In addition to the other works cited, see Cassirer on Carlyle's
view of the imagination (*Myth*, pp. 193–94). For the history of the
gradual ascendancy of the imagination over the reason in the eigh-
teenth century, see Ernest Lee Tuveson, *The Imagination as a
Means of Grace* (Berkeley: Univ. of California Press, 1960).

the thing in any way conceived as Visible" is a garment of the divine. Cannot man imagine whatever he wishes? Carlyle does not answer this kind of objection directly, but he does so implicitly by arguing that the senses ("Pains and Pleasures") are inferior to the imagination, that the Utilitarian view is a product of the lesser faculty, understanding. He insists that "not our Logical, mensurative faculty, but our Imaginative one is King over us" (p. 222). He continues: "Ever in the dullest existence there is a sheen either of Inspiration or of Madness (thou partly hast it in thy choice, which of the two), that gleams-in from the circumambient Eternity, and colours with its own hues our little islet of Time. The Understanding is indeed thy window, too clear thou canst not make it; but Fantasy is thy eye, with its colour-giving retina, healthy or diseased" (p. 222). Inspiration is thus linked to imagination and to the eye, Teufelsdröckh's most important organ. As I suggested earlier, inspiration for Carlyle is a working of the mind, not of something external to the mind on it. The mind must reach out to see the divine; the idea will not reach to touch the mind. The mind's eye can see only glimpses of the divine, but the exercise of the imagination, of the power to see, itself has a liberating and elevating effect on man. The ability of the imagination to range beyond what the understanding can know expands man's sense of what is possible for him and his sense of his power to overcome the apparent difficulties his understanding feels about him. What is possible nearly becomes what is imaginable.

Carlyle uses the reader's ability to imagine to rhetorical advantage. He not only talks about the power of the mind, but he also exercises it. He evokes an idea or image, then uses that act of imagination to make the reader both feel and believe in his power. For example, in "Natural Supernaturalism" Teufelsdröckh tries to diminish space and time to mere appearances. In what seems a fanciful aside he talks about Fortunatus's "wishing Hat," which annihilated space by whisking him where he wanted to go. Teufelsdröckh speculates on a time-annihilating hat: "This were indeed the grander: shooting at will from the Fire-Creation of the World to its Fire-Consummation; here historically present in the First Century, conversing face to face with Paul and Seneca; there prophetically in the Thirty-first, conversing also face to face with other Pauls and Senecas, who as yet stand hidden in the depth of that late Time!" Then Carlyle uses this idea of overcoming time, which we have accepted as an attractive fancy, to show us the true power we have over time: "Or thinkest thou it were impossible, unimaginable? Is the past annihilated, then, or only past; is the Future nonextant, or only future? Those mystic faculties of thine, Memory and Hope, already answer: already through those mystic avenues, thou the Earth-blinded summonest both Past and Future, and communest with them, though as yet darkly, and with mute beckonings" (p. 261). We cannot deny that our minds have a certain imaginative power over time. This feeling of power, and the hopefulness that accompanies it, is an important ingredient in the whole feeling Carlyle evokes in Book Third that we should act as if the world is as he describes it. He never allows us to feel that we can triumph completely over the phenomena that the senses direct to the understanding, but he does infect us with the possibility.

To aid the realization of the divine Idea in the world

our energies are directed to maintaining the appropriate symbols. Symbols, Teufelsdröckh explains, may have intrinsic or extrinsic value. The former are those fit for men to unite around. Of these the greatest are religious symbols and the "divinest" is "Jesus of Nazareth, and his Life, and his Biography, and what followed therefrom" (p. 224). But all symbols age, and even the "divinest" "will ever demand to be anew inquired into, and anew made manifest" (p. 224). The "Poet and inspired Maker . . . can shape new Symbols, and bring new Fire from Heaven to fix it there" (p. 225), but he who can discriminate and remove old symbols ranks as a "Legislator." Carlyle closes the chapter on Symbols very neatly by pointing to the "Champion of England" who can barely mount his horse as an example of a worn-out symbol. The picture of a withered aristocrat struggling vainly into the saddle is compelling, a concrete image of the need for social change.

In "Helotage" Carlyle uses Hofrath Heuschrecke, whose tract *Institute for the Repression of Population* the Editor conveniently digs up (p. 226), as a straw man in order to attack certain views on population.[16] What

[16] In "Carlyle, Jeffrey, and the 'Helotage' Chapter of *Sartor Resartus*," Alvan S. Ryan argues that this chapter is a serious lapse in Carlyle's handling of the "fictional element" in *Sartor* and that the chapter, which he sees, after Froude and D. A. Wilson, as an attack on Francis Jeffrey's ideas, has little relationship to the whole of *Sartor*. His argument depends on the apparent inconsistency of Carlyle's having Hofrath Heuschrecke, earlier portrayed as a fond disciple of Teufelsdröckh, write such a tract. No one has raised this objection before because readers respond to the consistency of the argument of the book, not to detailed consistency of characterization. Heuschrecke's development has not been made a matter of interest to us, and we are never forced to take him seriously as

Teufelsdröckh opposes is not simply Malthus's argument about the necessary expansion of the population,
but a whole view of the poor. The Editor summarizes
Heuschrecke's "deadly fear of Population" which Teufelsdröckh opposes: "Nowhere, in that quarter of his
intellectual world, is there light; nothing but a grim shadow of Hunger; open mouths opening wider and wider;
a world to terminate by the frightfullest consummation:
by its too dense inhabitants famished into delirium, universally eating one another. To make air for himself in
which strangulation, choking enough to a benevolent
heart, the Hofrath founds, or proposes to found, this
Institute of his, as the best he can do" (p. 227). Teufelsdröckh opposes this view by arguing for "human dig-
nity," by praising "the toilworn Craftsman that with
earth-made Implement laboriously conquers the Earth,
and makes her man's" (p. 227). The struggling of the
Craftsman parallels the higher activity of the Artist, "not
earthly craftsman only, but inspired Thinker" as well
(p. 228). Carlyle feels the poor man is blessed equally
with all, but fears "that the lamp of his soul should go
out; that no ray of heavenly, or even of earthly knowledge, should visit him" (p. 229). Knowledge should be
disseminated to all.

Carlyle then attacks Heuschrecke's Malthusianism
from a different point of view. In a satirical passage often
compared to Swift's "Modest Proposal," Teufelsdröckh
suggests hunting down paupers as a solution to the popu-

---

a character. We have not even heard of him since Book First. On
the other hand we may well be worried about population and not
really care that Councillor Grasshopper becomes a straw man, as
long as we are reassured about the future.

lation problem. Then he determines that a man is after all worth more than a horse. He finally decries the game-keeping aristocracy for not leading forth the masses in emigration to other lands. "Helotage" is an attack, not a very thorough or helpful one,[17] from several directions on a kind of Malthusian "deadly fear of Population," a rhetorical response to a point of view like that of Carlyle's friend Francis Jeffrey.[18] The chapter is, however, justified on more grounds than that of a desire to win a personal dispute, to convert a friend.

In its context "Helotage" meets and assuages the fears of a reader aroused by the leveling tendencies of the Clothes Philosophy. If anyone fears the poor, he will not be disposed toward a radical destruction and rebuilding of society. Furthermore, the Malthusian view of history is pessimistic and Carlyle's is optimistic. The spectre of population must be exorcised before the phoenix of a new and better society can rise from the ashes of the old. The place of "Helotage" in Book Third, just before "The Phoenix" is crucial. Like any good rhetorician Carlyle considers the disposition of his audience, as far as he can assess it, and frames his arguments accordingly. He saw in Jeffrey's arguments—if he had Jeffrey in mind, and he probably did—a kind of objection to his view which must be anticipated and met. In fact, as he frequently does, Carlyle arouses by the vivid use of language, a touch of the very fear he wishes to dispel. He presents the threat of hunger as a hideous apocalypse: "Nowhere, in that quarter of his intellectual world, is there light;

[17] See Harrold's note, *Sartor*, p. 226.
[18] See Jeffrey's letter of 13 November 1830 in D. A. Wilson, 2:106, quoted in part in Ryan's article, cited in note 14 above.

nothing but a grim shadow of Hunger; open mouths opening wider and wider; a world to terminate by the frightfullest consummation: by its too dense inhabitants, famished into delirium, universally eating one another." The
language is similar to that which Carlyle uses to describe
Teufelsdröckh's state of mind just prior to the Everlasting No (p. 166). In both cases the world threatens to de-
vour, and in both cases Carlyle vivifies the threat to increase the reader's desire to be free of it. And we may well
be grateful to and trusting of an orator who can lead us
out of fear.

We will need reassurance in the face of "The Phoenix."
Teufelsdröckh proclaims that society is dead, "the Poor
perishing, like neglected, foundered Draught-Cattle, of
Hunger and Over-work; the Rich, still more wretchedly,
of Idleness, Satiety, and Over-growth" (pp. 232–33). The
"Liberals, Economists, Utilitarians" are dancing over society's corpse (p. 233).[19] And, Teufelsdröckh insists, there
is nothing we can do to breathe life into society; we must
yield to "the Inevitable" (p. 235). The Editor accuses
Teufelsdröckh, as we well might independently, of encouraging the work of destruction, but the Editor puts
Teufelsdröckh's complicity in acceptable terms. The Professor, says the Editor, is "even willing that much should
be thrown to the Devil, so it were done but gently" (p.

[19] The reader committed to narrative consistency might ask
himself why Teufelsdröckh discusses specifically English problems. Does the reader choose to believe that there are German
"Motive Millwrights," "Liberals, Economists, Utilitarians"? Or is
Carlyle, to his discredit, inconsistent again? Of course his narrative is inconsistent, and the Englishness of the problems he exhorts
us to solve is one of the signs we have that the book is not essentially about German characters, but a persuasion directed at us.

235). Then Carlyle makes clear the fuller justification for letting society die. Society will be born again. The time and the conditions are uncertain, but "after, say two centuries of convulsion and conflagration, more or less vivid, the fire-creation should be accomplished, and we to find ourselves again in a Living Society, and no longer fighting but working" (p. 237). The ideal for society is the same as for the individual, a resolution and end of conflict in work.

The Editor closes the chapter remarking that "the judicious reader" may well expect Teufelsdröckh to show more respect to society, his "benefactress," who has after all "given not only food and raiment (of a kind), but books, tobacco and gukguk" (p. 237). Carlyle then hits right at the root of resistance to change, property,[20] allowing that the reader might expect also "less of a blind trust in the future, which resembles that rather of a philosophical Fatalist and Enthusiast, than of a solid householder paying scot-and-lot in a Christian country" (pp. 237–38).

At the beginning of "Old Clothes" Carlyle has the Editor assuage the feelings he has just taken into account at the end of "The Phoenix." Teufelsdröckh is a model of courtesy. He, "though a sanscullotist, is in practice probably the politest man extant." Teufelsdröckh himself

[20] Carlyle's friend Jeffrey wrote about the Reform agitation in the winter of 1830–1831: "The real battle is not between Whigs and Tories, Liberals and Illiberals and such gentlemen-like denominations, but between property and no property—Swing and the law," Jeffrey to Empson, 31 January 1831, quoted by Elie Halévy in *The Triumph of Reform, 1830–1841*, Vol. III of *A History of the English People in the Nineteenth Century*, tr. E. I. Watkin (New York: Barnes and Noble, 1961), p. 19.

remarks, "In Good-breeding, which differs, if at all, from High-breeding, only as it gracefully remembers the rights of others, rather than gracefully insists on its own rights, I discern no special connexion with wealth or birth: but rather that it lies in human nature itself, and is due from all men towards all men" (p. 238). Teufelsdröckh would surpass Dr. Johnson who bowed to every clergyman, by insisting that he would bow to every man, of whom he says: "is not he a Temple, then; the visible Manifestation and Impersonation of the Divinity" (p. 239). Carlyle does not remove the threat to property implicit in sansculottism, but by taking it into account and then insisting on Teufelsdröckh's profound and very flattering courtesy, he appears to remove any threat at all. What reader would allow himself to feel that he lacked natural "Goodbreeding" or that he could fail to admire it in his neighbors when "it gracefully remembers the rights of others"? (p. 238). The cause of leveling is advanced gently.

But it is advanced. On reflection we might well fear the apparently indiscriminate reverence Teufelsdröckh holds for all men. Carlyle, however, is several jumps ahead of us. He has Teufelsdröckh acknowledge that honoring men carelessly may appeal to the devil in them, to their vanity. Carlyle then pulls a dazzling ironic switch. He reinforces our sense of what should be honored by having Teufelsdröckh praise what many honor, but what should not be honored: "The gladder am I, on the other hand, to do reverence to those Shells and outer Husks of the Body, wherein no devilish passion any longer lodges, but only the pure emblem and effigies of Man: I mean, to Empty, or even to Cast Clothes. Nay, is it not to Clothes that most men do reverence: to the fine frogged broadcloth,

nowise to the 'straddling animal with bandy legs' which
it holds, and makes a Dignitary of? Who ever saw any
Lord my-lorded in tattered blanket fastened with wooden
skewer?" (pp. 239–40). Carlyle wishes to force on us
reverence not for the shell but for the kernel with all of
its fuming richness. We must accept men as they are, not
as their clothes make them. And Carlyle acknowledges
that the clothes are attractive: "The waistcoat hides no
evil passion, no riotous desire; hunger or thirst now
dwells not in it.Thus all is purged from the grossness of
sense, from the carking cares and foul vices of the World"
(p. 240). But the good must be taken with the bad. Monmouth Street is made an image of the variety of earthly
life, "where, in motley vision, the whole Pageant of Existence passes awfully before us; with its wail and jubi-
lee, mad loves and mad hatreds, church-bells and gal-
lows-ropes, farce-tragedy, beast-godhood,—the Bedlam
of Creation!"

The Editor remarks that "to most men, as it does to
ourselves, all this will seem overcharged" (p. 242), and
he shows that he takes Teufelsdröckh's wandering
through Monmouth Street quite literally by wishing for
records of the occasion. From the Editor's literal point of
view we understand that all of this *is* overcharged. We
understand as we read Teufelsdröckh's account of his
worship of clothes that it was overcharged, exaggerated,
ironic, yet that it contained great truth, to which "overcharged" is inadequate. Hats and waistcoats are free of
human failings, yet Monmouth Street is a foolish place
to worship. Clothing is only the husk of our experience,
but the image of heaps of clothing can move us to feel
what a bedlam creation is. The manner is agonistic, con-

sciously so, but its evocative power is strong, and the Editor's literal-mindedness forces us to evaluate its meaning precisely. As is often the case, the Editor's momentary dullness and inadequacy as a commentator calls attention to his own artificiality and the artificiality of the whole fictional apparatus of *Sartor*. He asks if it is not strange that, "in Paper-bag Documents destined for an English work, there exists nothing like an authentic diary of this his sojourn in London; and of his Meditations among the Clothes-shops only the obscurest emblematic shadows" (p. 243). The reader who has heard the flow of irony and truth in Teufelsdröckh's words will understand that he has not been talking literally about a trip into Monmouth Street. Nor will the reader react to the Editor's words by proclaiming that everything Teufelsdröckh does is symbolic, profound, and mysterious. The reader will rather take the Editor's tone and remarks as another manifestation of the subtle, playful, and ultimately serious voice of the implied orator. The nonsensical literalness of the Editor simply makes the implied orator more explicit than he is at other times.

In "Organic Filaments" Carlyle shows on what basis all men are united. The chapter is designed to subvert the old social hierarchy carefully and outline the new, all the while minimizing the threat of possible disorder.[21] Even in the burning of the "World-Phoenix," "organic

[21] In "Carlyle as Poet: The Phoenix Image in 'Organic Filaments,'" *VN*, No. 25 (spring 1964), Richard A. Levine says that the compact structure of the chapter "is, of course, a polemical organization. It begins with the statement of the problem and gradually builds argument upon argument, proof upon proof, until the final, and according to the logic of the work, ultimate conclusions" (p. 18).

filaments of the New mysteriously spin themselves" (p. 244). There is evidence of this spinning going on about us, for us, who will not live the two centuries required for the Phoenix cycle to be completed, to witness. We can see, for example, that we are all brothers, united by love or by necessity, by letters, spoken messages, and by minute influence on all men: "I say, there is not a red Indian, hunting by Lake Winnipic, can quarrel with his squaw, but the whole world must smart for it: will not the price of beaver rise?" (p. 246). We are also bound to men of the past, by tradition, by opinion and thought: "Thus all things wax, and roll onwards; Arts, Establishments, Opinions, nothing is completed, but ever completing" (p. 247). Even temporary destruction is a kind of progress: "The English Whig, has, in the second generation, become an English Radical; who, in the third again, it is to be hoped, will become an English Rebuilder" (p. 248). The Phoenix soars, then falls, that she may rise again.

The Editor makes the obvious reassuring comment: "Let the friends of social order, in such a disastrous period, lay this to heart, and derive from it any little comfort they can" (p. 248). The friends of social order must be braced for new shocks. Teufelsdröckh attacks titles of honor as a military anachronism that needs replacing by new and higher ones. He would preserve the title of King but insists his obedience is due only to the ruler "chosen for me in heaven" (p. 249).

The Editor wonders how the English with their politics of opposition and struggle can accommodate themselves to Teufelsdröckh's spiritual world. The Professor's serenity seems unworldly from the point of view of the English "in this spiritual Necropolis, or rather city both of the Dead and of the Unborn, where the present seems little other than an inconsiderable Film dividing the Past and the Future" (p. 249). Teufelsdröckh's radicalism seems awesome, and before the English reader is allowed to see the way out of darkness, he is subjected to a few more jolts. Teufelsdröckh scorns the ballot but allows it to stand on the shaky ground that if the English house is to be rebuilt from the top down, "what other, than the Representative Machine will serve your turn?" (p. 250). But the English are not free under this system. Further, the lower classes who desire war, apparently as a means to freedom, will only get themselves shot.

The path to freedom and light is hero worship. Freedom comes only through obedience, through religious loyalty, the foundation of all societies. The Editor looks about puzzled, allowing Carlyle to arrange Teufelsdröckh's argument to convince the most skeptical. If Paris could honor the aged Voltaire "in the most parched season of Man's History," can we not find heroes in a better season? The example prepares for Carlyle's plea for men of literature as the clergy-heroes of a quieter revolution than France's. Literature has its mendicant orders, its preaching friars or newspapermen, its prophet, Goethe, its communion of saints in the body of literature speaking of "Man's history, and Men's History, a perpetual Evangel. Listen, and for organ-music thou wilt ever, as of old, hear the Morning Stars sing together" (p. 254). Such radicalism need hardly be feared.

In "Natural Supernaturalism" Carlyle argues for an

attitude of wonder toward common things and "the divine miraculous course of human history" (p. 254). The course of his arguments is determined in part by the opposition to his point of view by "scientific individuals," and implicitly by Locke, Hume, and Voltaire.[22] Teufelsdröckh sets up his opposition by posing a series of their questions and answering them: What is a miracle? Is not a miracle simply a violation of the laws of nature? Does not nature operate by a constant set of rules? Are not these rules set down in the accumulated records of man's science?

The answer to these questions is that there are higher inexorable laws that man in his sphere of wondering ignorance cannot know. Teufelsdröckh asks, like God out of the whirlwind, if men were present at the creation. Man is a minnow in the ocean; he does not even know the alphabet of the volume of nature. Man's presumption to knowledge is one barrier to wonder and belief. Custom, which "Philosophy complains . . . has hoodwinked us" (p. 259), is another. Routine is valuable, but the mind need not be blind to the repeated presence of "the Stupendous" or to what lies above and beyond Custom (p. 259). Finally, Carlyle casts suspicion on what science or philosophy considers real, insisting madness has a claim on reality at least equal to that of the nerves. Carlyle then uses the imagination, in a passage discussed above, to free man momentarily from the restrictions of space and time. What the imagination sees allows belief, not un-

[22] See Harrold, *Sartor*, p. 257, n. 1, p. 259n; Holmberg, "David Hume in Carlyle's *Sartor Resartus*"; and the response to Voltaire in "The Everlasting Yea," discussed above in chapter 4.

derstanding. With God all is here and now, and men are spirits passing quickly through this life from eternity to eternity, but not passive spirits:

Thus, like a God-created, fire-breathing Spirit-host, we emerge from the Inane; haste stormfully across the astonished Earth; then plunge again into the Inane. Earth's mountains are levelled, and her seas filled up, in our passage: can the Earth, which is but dead and a vision, resist Spirits which have reality and are alive? On the hardest adamant some footprint of us is stamped-in; the last Rear of the host will read traces of the earliest Van. But whence?—O Heaven, whither? Sense knows not; Faith knows not; only that it is through Mystery to Mystery, from God and to God.

[pp. 266–67]

Teufelsdröckh's rhetoric makes us feel ourselves Titan-spirits, mysterious, wonderful, and powerful. Infected with this attitude we are bound to act and feel as if history can be molded to our will, which of course is only a manifestation of a higher will. In summing up our progress in "Circumspective," the Editor asks rhetorically, "In a word, do we at length stand safe in the far region of Poetic Creation and Palingenesia, where that Phoenix Death-Birth of Human Society, and of all Human Things appears possible, is seen to be inevitable?" (p. 268). Again, the imaginable becomes the real. With this metaphysical understanding, the kinds of action, or attitude toward social change, which have been urged explicitly and implicitly throughout Book Third and the whole of *Sartor* should seem both right and easy.

The believing reader who feels wonder about him has, the Editor explains, an obligation to speak his thankfulness to Teufelsdröckh "in many a Tea-circle" and to look

down upon "Codification and Political Economy, and the
Theory of the British Constitution" from the perspective
of the Clothes Science (p. 270). For the reader still unsure
of the implications of the Clothes Philosophy, who wishes
something useful for his money, the Editor presents two
practical inferences in "The Dandiacal Body" and "Tailors." These two chapters are a final attempt to set right
society's inverted values. As the Editor says, in regard to
dandies and tailors, "it may be asserted without scruple,
that the public feeling, unenlightened by Philosophy, is
at fault; and even that the dictates of humanity are violated" (p. 271). Such seriousness, however, is often
implicit rather than explicit in these two chapters, which
are spirited and humorous, and dawns only gradually on
the reader.

In the first chapter, "The Dandiacal Body," Carlyle
comes very close to self-parody. The result is humorous
and effective, because it is Carlyle's intention to show that
the dandy is indeed a false parody of the believer in the
Clothes Philosophy. The irony of the first section of the
chapter is close to that of "Old Clothes" where Teufelsdröckh insists untruthfully that he worships clothes, the
husks or shells of our existence. Here the Editor defines
the dandy:

A Dandy is a Clothes-wearing Man, a Man whose trade, office,
and existence consists in the wearing of Clothes. Every faculty
of his soul, spirit, purse, and person is heroically consecrated
to this one object, the wearing of Clothes wisely and well:
so that as others dress to live, he lives to dress. The all-
importance of Clothes, which a German Professor, of un-
equalled learning and acumen, writes his enormous Volume
to demonstrate, has sprung up in the intellect of the Dandy

without effort, like an instinct of genius; he is inspired with Cloth, a Poet of Cloth. What Teufelsdröckh would call a "Divine Idea of Cloth" is born with him; and this, like other such Ideas, will express itself outwardly, or wring his heart asunder with unutterable throes.

[p. 272]

The transition from this apparent mockery of dandies to a much more serious statement about English society is affected in part by the transition from the Editor's voice, which in this passage is hardly distinguishable, but for the context, from Teufelsdröckh's voice. The Editor says simply that now that we have the science of the Clothes Philosophy we can analyze "the essential nature of the British Dandy, and the mystic significance that lies in him" (p. 274). This proposal looks like an excuse for more humor at the dandy's expense, since implicit in the Editor's ironic treatment of him is the feeling that the dandy has no "mystic significance," is only shell and no kernel. But we underestimate Carlyle, for he wishes us to feel the deep significance of the materialism the dandy represents.

As I have suggested all along, the temptation to try to understand the use of the Editor in circumstances like this in terms of character development will only lead to confusion. Here the Editor talks like Teufelsdröckh and speaks ironically in a way consistent with what the whole book has made us feel is the truth. Are we to feel that he does not understand his own irony? And what does it mean that he is now contributing two chapters of his own to his *Sartor Resartus*? Is he so completely converted he can now spread Teufelsdröckh's message as he pleases?

And speak ironically? When did his conversion take place? We simply do not have grounds to answer these questions, nor is there any indication in the book that we should even ask them, much less try to answer them. As we read, we understand the immediate relevance of what the Editor says, and unless we are predisposed to approach the book as a novel, we will not reflect backward and forward on the Editor's character.

Teufelsdröckh's analysis succeeds in showing, with growing seriousness, how dandyism is institutionalized and is a false and predominating sect. The analysis proceeds with an ingenious mixture of whimsy and sound sense. Teufelsdröckh insists that the religious principle is manifest in nineteenth-century England in the form of dandyism. He relates it to historically antecedent sects and shows that dandies have the zeal and separatist tendencies of all new sects. They have their temples, high priests, and rites. Their sacred books are *"Fashionable Novels."* Carlyle here joins the attacks begun in *Fraser's* on the novel and on Bulwer's *Pelham* in particular. The Professor claims to know *Pelham* through a kind of dissertation on fashionable novels found on "a defaced stray-sheet, probably the outcast fraction of some English Periodical, such as they name *Magazine*" (p. 278).[23] Teufelsdröckh derives the seven "Articles of Faith" of

[23] In claiming to know *Pelham* through an English magazine, Teufelsdröckh may speak quite literally of Carlyle's own situation. The seven "Articles of Faith" are contained in excerpts from *Pelham* quoted in the second of two reviews of fashionable novels in *Fraser's*. See *Fraser's*, 1 (1830), 517–18. The first review is in *Fraser's*, 1, 318–35. Matthew Whiting Rosa in *The Silver Fork School* says that Carlyle is not fair to *Pelham* (p. 19). It seems unlikely that Carlyle had read *Pelham*.

dandyism from *Pelham*. The seriousness of the vanity
these articles of faith represent becomes clearly evident
when the dandy is contrasted with another English sect,
the drudges. Teufelsdröckh's analysis of the drudges
parallels that of the dandies. The drudges have their cos-
tumes and rites, but the darkness of suffering and want
shows through the glib analysis. The full contrast between the two sects becomes perfectly clear in the descriptions of a "Poor-Slave Household" and a "Dandiacal
Household."[24] What seemed a clever game, a parody of
Clothes-Science becomes serious:

Such are the two Sects which, at this moment, divide the more
unsettled portion of the British People; and agitate that ever-
vexed country. To the eye of the political Seer, their mutual
relation, pregnant with the elements of discord and hostility,
is far from consoling. These two principles of Dandiacal Self-
worship or Demon-worship, and Poor-Slavish or Drudgical
Earth-worship, or whatever that same Drudgism may be, do
as yet indeed manifest themselves under distant and nowise
considerable shapes: nevertheless, in their roots and subter-
ranean ramifications, they extend through the entire structure
of Society, and work unweariedly in the secret depths of
English national Existence; striving to separate and isolate it
into two contradictory, uncommunicating masses.

[p. 285]

[24] The "Dandiacal Household," from the introduction to Bulwer's *The Disowned*, was also quoted in *Fraser's*, 1 (1830), 515, as
MacMechan indicates in his *Sartor*, p. 392, n. 258, 12. As Harrold
notes (*Sartor*, p. 283n), the description of the "Poor-Slave Household" is quoted with minor changes from John Bernard, *Retrospec-
tions of the English Stage* (London: H. Colburn and R. Bentley,
1830), I, 349–50. A sentence Carlyle dropped from the end of Bernard's description indicates the kind of complacency Carlyle was
attacking: "They ate as Nature dictated, and as God had given;—
they ate, and were satisfied" (p. 350). Also quoted by MacMechan,
p. 392, n. 257, 9.

The rich and the poor divide the nation and will continue to divide it further, if left alone.

Carlyle chooses to suggest the possible outcome of such division only briefly, through two vivid figures. The two groups are two expanding whirlpools which may eat up all intermediate land and meet: "And then—we have the true Hell of Waters, and Noah's Deluge is outdeluged!" They are electrical poles, one gathering all the positive electricity, money, and the other the negative, hunger. If they meet: "The Earth is but shivered into impalpable smoke by that Doom's-thunderpeal; the Sun misses one of his Planets in Space, and thenceforth there are no eclipses of the Moon" (pp. 286–87).

These examples of the two sects that divide are a crucial part of Carlyle's argument. They present what Richard M. Weaver in *The Ethics of Rhetoric* would call an argument from circumstances;[25] and as Carlyle framed them, they depend for their effect on what Frank Kermode has called "the sense of an ending."[26] The argument is circumstantial in an obvious sense. It tells us that we must act to remedy a bad situation, which if left uncorrected will lead to worse consequences. The will to act is encouraged by Carlyle's apocalyptic rhetoric, a favorite mode of argument. The consequences of inertia will be cosmic. Of course, as Carlyle implies throughout all of *Sartor*, so will the consequences of action, according to the principles of the Clothes Philosophy, be cosmic.

[25] See "Edmund Burke and the Argument from Circumstance," in *The Ethics of Rhetoric* (Chicago: Henry Regnery Co., 1953), pp. 55–84.

[26] *The Sense of an Ending: Studies in the Theory of Fiction* (New York: Oxford Univ. Press, 1967).

Carlyle gives us an exaggerated sense of our power over the future, in our action or in our inaction.

Carlyle uses the Editor to break off this dark vision, claiming that he is tired of "likenings and similitudes" and that the Professor perhaps has clouded vision. Teufelsdröckh's vision is of course perfectly clear, and the Editor calls attention to that fact rather awkwardly by asking if there has not been some satire in what Teufelsdröckh has said. Some will object, the Editor says, that the Professor takes them for simpletons: "His irony has overshot itself; we see through it, and perhaps through him" (p. 287). Indeed we do. The Editor again forces us to look through the fictions to the implied orator, to the intention at work in all of the material of *Sartor*.

The second practical deduction, "Tailors," attempts to readjust English values by calling for due attention to the true moral and social leaders. Carlyle does this elliptically and quickly, counting on the reader's familiarity with his central ideas. The tailor is not simply a destroyer but a creator, as are those metaphorical tailors, poets. Real tailors, like the "Breeches-Maker to his Majesty" should look forward to a better day, "a day of justice, when the worth of Breeches would be revealed to man, and the Scissors become forever venerable" (p. 291). Implicit in this imperative is all that Carlyle has said about the importance to society and the individual of clothes symbols, the need to replace worn symbols with new ones more appropriate to the divine idea behind them, to concern oneself with the kernel not the husk of existence, to honor those who lead in the process of destroying and recreating society.

In "Farewell" Carlyle has the Editor summarize the

possible effect of the book and apologize for and explain certain qualities of Teufelsdröckh's manner that might be objected to. The book has perhaps added "some morsel of spiritual nourishment . . . to the scanty ration of our beloved British world" (p. 292). Even what appears to be an apology for Teufelsdröckh's rhetorical intention, his desire to proselytize, is turned to rhetorical advantage, to an actual exhortation for men to unite under and proselytize for the Clothes Philosophy. Men can help men in the fight against the monsters, hypocrisy, atheism, and sensuality. Then Carlyle uses one other typical, striking effect. News comes that Teufelsdröckh has parted from Weissnichtwo, leaving behind him a sense that the Clothes revolution has begun, that the Parisian Three Days and the Saint-Simonians are signs of its start. Teufelsdröckh's presence is not known, but the Editor guesses "Teufelsdröckh is actually in London!" (p. 297). The Professor moves with the action, and the reader feels the revolution must be heading for England. In addition, the careful reader has felt nearly from the beginning that the Teufelsdröckh who wrote the real *Sartor Resartus* for *Fraser's* was in fact in London all along. If he has not yet decided, the reader has the whole complex problem of how seriously to take the fictions of *Sartor* dumped directly in his lap.

The book closes with an astute anticipation of the "irritancy and even spoken invective" the book met in *Fraser's* (p. 297). In the last sentence Carlyle uses that possible antagonism to score one more rhetorical victory: "Have we not, in the course of Eternity, travelled some months of our Life-journey in partial sight of one another; have we not existed together, though in a state of quarrel?" (p. 298). As he has argued before, men are bound to one another even by animosity. How can we deny him?

In sum, *Sartor Resartus* is a unique persuasive work. Carlyle urges the truths he knows through fictional devices that permit him to achieve a variety of agonistic but effective rhetorical maneuvers, in all of which we see Carlyle, the implied orator, urging us to believe in and act on the Clothes Philosophy. The work progresses carefully through a series of arguments for elements of the Clothes Philosophy, taking into account and attempting to control the reader's intellectual and emotional response to these ideas. Book First presents the fictional devices and implicit mode of speaking of the book. It then begins the argument of the whole work by suggesting that things of this earth are unreal, mere products of the senses, and can be overcome by the imagination, which can glimpse the eternal realities beyond. Man has the creative power of imagination but is also restricted by what he creates, by the organically aging symbols in which he tries to embody spiritual realities. Man ought, then, to change the symbols by which he lives, especially the crucial symbols that determine social organization. Carlyle places Book Second, Teufelsdröckh's biography, at this point. Book Second substantiates the Clothes Philosophy, connects it with the personal situation of the reader, and moves him to a willingness to accept the world and to act in it to create a new society. Book Third confirms aspects of the Clothes Philosophy stated briefly and tentatively in Book First, directs the reader's willingness to act, and applies the Clothes Philosophy to the immediate social situation of England. *Sartor* is a complete and coherent act of persuasion.

6: Considerations and Conclusions

A CONSIDERATION of the form of *Sartor* is bound to provoke the question of why Carlyle chose to preach his Clothes Philosophy in such an unusual and complex book. The causes of a work of literature are manifold, and some of the causes of *Sartor* can only be hinted at here. Carlyle himself anticipates wonder at the complexity and eccentricity of his book in its last chapter. The Editor regrets "this piebald, entangled, hyper-metaphorical style of writing, not to say of thinking" (p. 293), as it appears both in Teufelsdröckh's and his own writing. Teufelsdröckh's attitude is admirable; he has warred with the devil from birth: "Still the question returns on us: How could a man occasionally of keen insight, not without keen sense of propriety, who had real Thoughts to communicate, resolve to emit them in a shape bordering so closely on the absurd?" (p. 293). This is precisely the question which has bothered some critics of *Sartor*, not just critics of Teufelsdröckh.

I have argued that the book is a coherent work of persuasion. Still, one may ask why it is such a complex work of persuasion. The Editor offers his guess: "Our conjecture has sometimes been, that perhaps Necessity as well as Choice was concerned in it. Seems it not conceivable that, in a Life like our Professor's, where so much bountifully given by Nature had in Practice failed and misgone,

Literature also would never rightly prosper: that striving with his characteristic vehemence to paint this and the other Picture, and ever without success, he at last desperately dashes his sponge, full of all colours, against the canvas, to try whether it will paint Foam?" (p. 294). The Editor offers a second explanation: "It is, that Teufelsdröckh is not without some touch of the universal feeling, a wish to proselytize. How often already have we paused, uncertain whether the basis of this so enigmatic nature were really Stoicism and Despair, or Love and Hope only seared into the figure of these!" (p. 294). These passages lead us again out of the book and into the circumstances under which *Sartor* was written. The style of writing and thinking which the Editor apologizes for is not, as we have seen, exclusively Teufelsdröckh's, and we have no recourse but to think that the author is telling us something about the conditions under which he wrote. As we have seen, Carlyle tended to account for the particular form of *Sartor* in terms of his isolation in Craigenputtock, his unfamiliarity with his audience, and the limitations of contemporary publications and their readers. Carlyle felt he had to speak, to "proselytize," and he felt that in creating this form, he was adapting to difficult conditions.

This explanation of the form of *Sartor* is some help in evaluating it. We can perceive that he used unusual means and conventions that were available in order to reach an audience of which he was uncertain. In doing so, he created an original, complex work. Others before him, as the prospectus of *Fraser's Magazine* points out, had used fictional devices as a means of "shifting off any individual responsibility."[1] Yet none had sustained those devices and the style associated with them as Carlyle does. The choices he made, especially that of using fictional devices, made his work more complex than it might have been; but as we have seen, he created for himself a variety of rhetorical advantages.

By choosing to use fictional devices, Carlyle also imposed certain restrictions on the subsequent choices he made in presenting his ideas. These restrictions do not outweigh the advantages he creates, but they are worth noticing, particularly because of their relevance to problems of form. The fictional devices in *Sartor* help determine the form of the book, but they do not control that form. I have argued that Carlyle does not interest us in his fictions in such a way that interest in them is an end in itself and usurps our interest in the Clothes Philosophy. Using fictions and apparent narrative without diverting the reader's interest to character and plot is difficult, and Carlyle shows an awareness of that difficulty in his constant efforts to point out both the deeper intention of his work and the artificiality of his fictions. The tendency of modern critics to focus on the fictions as the matter of crucial interest is a tribute to the strength of modern novelistic criticism and to the critics' worthy intention to rescue *Sartor* from those who insist that the book is not art. Their concern with the fictional devices is not, however, a mark of Carlyle's failure to preserve priorities in *Sartor*.

As in the case of the Editor's guess that Teufelsdröckh is in London, the reader's perception of Carlyle's fictions

[1] "Our 'Confession of Faith,'" *Fraser's*, 1 (1930), 1.

is subject to remarkable manipulations. At one moment
Teufelsdröckh is obviously only a surrogate for an English author talking about English problems. At another he
is a German talking about England from a distance. At
still another he is a typical romantic hero. The human
imagination seems capable of astonishing shifts in belief.
In reading *Sartor*, the mind seems absolutely untroubled
at being told one moment that a character named Devil's
Dung is merely a humorous disguise for an anonymous
author, or for Carlyle if the secret is out, and at the next
moment that as a boy he carried his supper outdoors and
ate it on the orchard wall (pp. 92–93). The boy is perfectly real in our imaginations, and we do not insist that
he represent Carlyle as a boy sitting on a similar wall in
Ecclefechan.

The kind of consistency our minds demand, as I have
suggested before, is a consistency of rhetorical presentation of the Clothes Philosophy. But this is not a sufficient
explanation. If Teufelsdröckh and the Editor disappeared,
and Carlyle continued preaching the Clothes Philosophy,
we would feel that consistency had been violated. Such
is not always the case with the use of fictional devices like
the ones in *Sartor*.

Carlyle frequently begins his essays with some manner of pretense, some fictional author; but often this
pretense is merely conventional, an excuse for a heightened oratorical tone, and the reader is aware only of
Thomas Carlyle, or an anonymous voice, conducting an
argument. In "On History Again," for example, the
headnote alone calls attention to the "D. T." who sup-
posedly wrote the piece. After that the pretense is
dropped; the reader is not aware that he is reading any-

thing other than an essay by Thomas Carlyle (*Works*, 28:167–76). On the other hand, fictional devices like that at the beginning of "On History Again" seem to be a natural way of establishing a basis for written, as opposed to spoken, rhetoric. In oral delivery, the conditions of the speech are usually set by the time, place, and occasion. In written delivery, some fiction, or better pretense, is often needed to establish for the reader the manner and conventions with which he is to be addressed. Milton's "Areopagitica" is not really an address to Parliament and will remain untouched and unchanged if the reader recognizes that Milton is pretending. Deceit is not an issue. Similarly, Burke's *Reflections on the Revolution in France* is not a letter to a young Frenchman, but for Burke the pretense that it is a letter is a ground for his rhetoric.[2] The difference between *Sartor* and these two examples seems to be one of degree.

Some persuasive essays employing fiction or pretense do not require constant maintenance of that fiction. On the other hand, in cases other than *Sartor*, the continued presence of fictions is demanded in order to preserve the

---

[2] Burke says that the *Reflections* began in correspondence, that a second letter was requested of him, which grew too long and required more detailed development than a letter allowed: "However, having thrown down his first thoughts in the form of a letter, and indeed, when he sat down to write, having intended it for a private letter, he found it difficult to change the form of address, when his sentiments had grown into a greater extent, and had received another direction. A different plan, he is sensible, might be more favourable to a commodious division and distribution of his matter." See *Reflections on the Revolution in France*, Vol. IV of *The Works of the Right Honourable Edmund Burke*, ed. F. W. Rafferty, The World's Classics (London: Oxford Univ. Press, 1907), p. 2.

internal consistency of the work. In Dryden's *Essay of Dramatic Poesy*, for example, where characters have a kind of fullness and consistency they lack in *Sartor* (Dryden is more genuinely skeptical), the pretense of false names, separate characters, and a boat ride must be maintained. If Dryden drops the pretense and continues the piece as an essay on drama, the reader will feel he has violated the rules of the game. The fictions in *Sartor* establish conditions for Carlyle's rhetoric and must be maintained, but only according to the manner in which they are defined from the first. In a way, as Carlisle Moore argues in "Thomas Carlyle and Fiction," *Sartor* has the consistency of a hoax; it remains what it is. But one must see exactly what it is. It is not a representation of an Editor editing German materials at all. In that case the hoax would be a form of narrative fiction, a representation of an Englishman pretending to edit foreign material he has created himself. *Sartor* is rather an attempt to persuade the reader to believe in and act by the Clothes Philosophy by means of a fictional editor, a fictional German professor, and other fictional devices. It is a mode of speaking implicitly. What must remain consistent is both the persuasive intention and the means by which it is conveyed. The flexibility available within this framework is quite great. The artificiality of the fictions may be pointed to, or they may be made real, as long as they are consistent with the persuasive intention and are not discarded altogether.[3]

What Carlyle may not do is drop his fictions and speak

[3] Carlisle Moore seems close to this point of view when he says that *Sartor* instructs "by deceiving unsuccessfully" ("Thomas Carlyle and Fiction, 1822–1834," p. 152).

to the reader in his own voice. We become accustomed very soon to knowing him implicitly and expect him to continue in that manner. The fictions, then, are what keeps *Sartor* from being what many have been tempted to call it, a work of exhortation that speaks directly out of personal experience, a work like *Walden*.[4] The distinction between these two kinds of works is a very subtle one because certainly at moments we feel we are reading what Henry Larkin calls "intense, unmitigated Carlyle."[5] The distinction does not lie at all, however, in the intensity of what is said. If anything, Carlyle's fictions allow him to intensify the way he addresses the reader. The difference between *Sartor* and a work like *Walden* lies in the way in which we interpret what is said to us. Thoreau, speaking in his own voice, must speak the truth and must convince us that his knowledge and experience justify what he says. Carlyle, on the other hand, by representing fictional experience, by rhetorical exaggeration in the mouth of a Professor we know is fictional, can evoke responses that may be greater than or different from

[4] Perry Miller in his "Afterword" to the Signet Classic edition of *Walden* (New York: New American Library, 1960), has located this quality in *Walden*. He says that after rereading the book "the reader discovers a key to its riddle in the form of Thoreau's address to him. While the account purports to be the solitary meditations or reminiscences of a hermit beside a pond of water, the prose is actually written in the rhythms of public speech. Thoreau is not musing, he is orating. When he addresses the reader as 'you,' he is not speaking softly to one person, but haranguing multitudes. Look, for instance, at the summons in Chapter 2 to 'Simplify, simplify.' One cannot read that paragraph quietly any more than one can murmur a speech of Daniel Webster's" (p. 252).

[5] *Carlyle and the Open Secret of His Life* (London: Kegan Paul, 1886), p. 35.

what he could create in response to his own voice and to his own unfictionalized experience. It is true that we then weigh this response to fiction against our response to the implied orator, against what we have come to understand as his mind and, as far as we can know it, his knowledge and experience, so that ultimately we have a similar check on what is said. This second method appears capable of much greater suggestibility or evocative power, but is much more hazardous and difficult. There is always the chance that the implied orator's mind and experience will not support the responses evoked. If it will not, the reader will be aware of the straining after unsubstantiated truths. When a man speaking in his own voice misstates his experience, we can have the satisfaction of calling him a liar or a fool, but we should feel at least some remote sympathy for his predicament. Yet when an orator speaks implicitly, through fictions, what pretends to be the truth and is unsupported, we feel almost nothing at all.

By using fictions, Carlyle expands greatly the rhetorical resources available to him, and he gains the lure of eccentricity. He can exaggerate, understate, misstate, speak ironically or seriously, all the while controlling the reader's apprehension of what he is doing. He can use the reader's naive curiosity about fictions and his amusement with self-conscious make-believe. Carlyle creates for the reader an original reading experience, which acquires additional value through its uniqueness.

For some readers, of course, the range of rhetorical devices, the implicit mode of speaking, the difficulty of the work, and, perhaps, the nature of Carlyle's ideas make the work ineffective and often enough unreadable. There can be no doubt that it was effective for great numbers of nineteenth-century readers, but the book, especially when its novelty has worn off, demands more of modern readers. The extent to which it speaks to a particular, historical condition of the spirit will limit its effectiveness in time. One can argue that its appeal is universal, but clearly much of its reference is particular. The growing need for profuse footnotes to the text cannot be ignored. One must wonder, then, why we should burden ourselves, in capacities other than those of scholars and historians, and burden our students with works of persuasion directed to audiences long dead. Why should a modern reader, especially one like John Muirhead, who finds holes in Carlyle's logic, encourage others to read *Sartor*?

One kind of judgment can be made of *Sartor*. In the role of what Aristotle calls "observers," we can declare that the orator is very skillful, that he uses well what rhetorical resources are available to him. But, we might ask, of what value, other than as a model, is a clever work of persuasion if it does not persuade us? Why should subsequent generations be bothered with works intended to move their ancestors to belief and action? The answer lies, I think, in the ability of certain works of persuasion to move men to a kind of momentary, imaginative belief. Although many of us may not conduct ourselves as Carlyle wished, we can be moved by *Sartor*. To be moved to imaginative (but nonetheless real) assent by such a work of persuasion is of permanent value because it is an act of sympathy. For a moment we see the world from an alien point of view, through a fellow man's eyes. That is the value of the best works of persuasion. We see for a mo-

ment the consequences of belief and assess them for ourselves, for the speaker, and perhaps for all men. This
imaginative insight may bring relief, elevation, or despair. Several conditions seem necessary for this experience to take place. We must feel that the truths of which
we are being persuaded are significant, worthy at least of
human consideration. We are likely to think that they are
significant if they relate to permanent problems. We
must know either directly or intuitively that the truths
have human consequences in the real world. The extraordinary accomplishment of *Sartor* is that it creates the
feeling in the reader that the Clothes Philosophy is rele-
vant to the condition of men in the real world in spite of
its fictions, in spite of particular reference, and without
the constantly functioning analogous world a novel or an
apologue employs. As the Editor tells us, our stake in the
Clothes Philosophy is real. These ideas must be assessed
in terms of our world, our lives. We feel the effect that I
have called the "implied orator," a single, controlling human voice speaking to us about human experience. And
in the face of the "Everlasting Yea" or the ominous warning of the last chapters, we may give momentary assent
and feel in the first case the joyous certainty that comes
with the acceptance of duty and in the second case a
sympathetic urge to get about our work to prevent social
chaos. We know what Carlyle is talking about.[6]

The condition to which Carlyle speaks most directly is

---

[6] See Ralph W. Rader's discussion of the differences between
fictional and factual works and of the literary qualities of factual
works, the category in which I have argued *Sartor* should be
placed, in his "Literary Form in Factual Narrative: The Example
of Boswell's *Johnson*."

that of young men. The world is bad enough for all men: "Nevertheless, in these sick days, when the Born of Heaven first descries himself (about the age of twenty) in a world such as ours, richer than usual in two things, in Truths grown obsolete, and Trades grown obsolete,— what can the fool think but that it is all a Den of Lies, wherein whoso will not speak Lies and act Lies, must stand idle and despair?" (p. 156). If this predicament is not permanent, it is at least recurrent. The direction in which *Sartor* stirs young men, to action, to work, to attention to duty, may seem indiscriminate and open to manipulation, but it is at least a stirring; and as Carlyle directs it in *Sartor*, it is a stirring to awareness of the disparity between rich and poor, which can hardly be belittled today.

As the dandy reappears among us and the poor slave reappears in city ghettoes, *Sartor* seems less and less antique. Carlyle's work as a whole is being reappraised and his analyses of social problems admired, even if his solutions are not.[7] If at a minimum we can only sympathize with his prospect of ultimate solutions, we can certainly learn from his insight into our failings. Yet, regardless of the permanent effects of his ideas upon us, there re-

[7] See Cassirer, *Myth*; Daiches, *Carlyle and the Victorian Dilemma*; Leo Marx, *The Machine in the Garden: Technology and the Pastoral Ideal in America* (New York: Oxford Univ. Press, 1964), esp. pp. 170–90; Raymond Williams, "Thomas Carlyle," in *Culture and Society, 1780–1950* (New York: Columbia Univ. Press, 1958), pp. 71–86; Herbert Sussman, "Transcendentalism and the Machine: Thomas Carlyle," in *Victorians and the Machine: The Literary Response to Technology* (Cambridge, Mass.: Harvard Univ. Press, 1968), pp. 13–40; Albert J. LaValley, *Carlyle and the Idea of the Modern*.

mains the rich experience of reading *Sartor*. Carlyle's rhetorical art will continue to provoke wonder, and at least momentary new hope, through imaginative submission to a lively, eccentric orator with important ideas about the human condition.

The historical importance of *Sartor* is beyond question. Though it met with disfavor when it was first published serially in *Fraser's Magazine*, once it was published as a book it became gradually a popular and effective work. In 1882 *Sartor* sold 70,000 copies, and it went through nine editions as late as 1900.[8] Discussing the work's slow rise to fame, the historian William Edward Hartpole Lecky remarked in 1891 that "it has penetrated far and wide through all classes, and it is now, I suppose, one of the most popular and influential of the books that were published in England in the second quarter of the century."[9] As Carlyle soon found out, it had its greatest effect on young men, like his former pupil Charles Buller, Froude, and even young minds as unlike Carlyle's as T. H. Huxley's.[10] Carlyle's influence on the Victorian pe-

[8] Richard D. Altick, *The English Common Reader: A Social History of the Mass Reading Public, 1800–1900* (Chicago: Univ. of Chicago Press, 1957), p. 390; Julian Symons, *Thomas Carlyle: The Life and Ideas of a Prophet* (London: Victor Gollancz, 1952), p. 129.

[9] "Carlyle's Message to his Age," in *Historical and Political Essays* (New York: Longmans, Green, 1910), pp. 95–96. First printed in *Contemporary Review*, 1891.

[10] See letter to John Carlyle, 10 January 1832 (*Letters*, p. 287); Froude, *Thomas Carlyle, A History of His Life in London*, I, 246–52; and William Irvine, "Carlyle and T. H. Huxley," in *Booker Memorial Studies: Eight Essays on Victorian Literature in Memory of John Manning Booker, 1881–1948*, ed. Hill Shine (Chapel Hill: Univ. of North Carolina Press, 1950), pp. 104–21, reprinted in *Victorian Literature: Modern Essays in Criticism*, ed. Austin Wright, Galaxy Book (New York: Oxford Univ. Press, 1961), 193–207.

riod was profound; and through the particular mode of *Sartor*, he spoke to English readers with special force. In 1855 George Eliot said of Carlyle, "For there is hardly a superior or active mind of this generation that has not been modified by Carlyle's writing; there has hardly been an English book written for the last ten or twelve years that would not have been different if Carlyle had not lived. The character of his influence is best seen in the fact that many of the men who have the least agreement with his opinions are those to whom the reading of *Sartor Resartus* was an epoch in the history of their minds."[11] That is high praise indeed.

[11] "Thomas Carlyle," in *Essays of George Eliot*, ed. Thomas Pinney (London: Routledge and K. Paul, 1963), pp. 213–14.

Selected Bibliography

THOMAS CARLYLE

Carlyle's Unfinished History of German Literature. Ed. Hill Shine. Lexington: Univ. of Kentucky Press, 1951.

Correspondence Between Goethe and Carlyle. Ed. Charles Eliot Norton. London: Macmillan, 1887.

The Correspondence of Emerson and Carlyle. Ed. Joseph Slater. New York: Columbia Univ. Press, 1964.

The Last Words of Thomas Carlyle. New York: D. Appleton and Co., 1892.

Letters of Thomas Carlyle, 1826–1836. Ed. Charles Eliot Norton. 2 vols. London: Macmillan, 1888.

The Letters of Thomas Carlyle to His Brother Alexander. Ed. Edwin W. Marrs, Jr. Cambridge, Mass.: Belknap Press of Harvard Univ. Press, 1968.

Letters of Thomas Carlyle to John Stuart Mill, John Sterling, and Robert Browning. Ed. Alexander Carlyle. New York: Frederick A. Stokes Co., 1923.

Letters of Thomas Carlyle to William Graham. Ed. John Graham, Jr. Princeton: Princeton Univ. Press, 1950.

The Love Letters of Thomas Carlyle and Jane Welsh. Ed. Alexander Carlyle. 2 vols. London: John Lane, 1909.

"New Letters of Carlyle to Eckermann." Ed. William A. Speck. *Yale Review,* 15 (July 1926), 736–57.

New Letters of Thomas Carlyle. Ed. Alexander Carlyle. 2 vols. London: John Lane, 1904.

Reminiscences by Thomas Carlyle. Ed. Charles Eliot Norton. 2 vols. London: Macmillan, 1887.

Reminiscences by Thomas Carlyle. Ed. James Anthony Froude. 2 vols. New York: Harper, 1881.

"Sartor Resartus." *Fraser's Magazine* (London: J. Fraser), 8 (Nov., Dec. 1833), 581–92, 669–84; 9 (Feb., March, April,

June 1834), 177–95, 301–13, 443–55, 664–74; 10 (July, Aug. 1834), 77–87, 182–93.

Sartor Resartus: The Life and Opinions of Herr Teufels-dröckh. London: Saunders and Otley, 1838.

Sartor Resartus: The Life and Opinions of Herr Teufels-dröckh. Vol. I of *Collected Works of Thomas Carlyle.* Library Edition. 30 vols. London: Chapman and Hall, 1869–71.

Sartor Resartus: The Life and Opinions of Herr Teufels-dröckh. Ed. Charles Frederick Harrold. New York: Odyssey Press, 1937.

Two Note Books of Thomas Carlyle from 23d March 1822 to 16th May 1832. Ed. Charles Eliot Norton. New York: Grolier Club, 1898.

The Works of Thomas Carlyle. Ed. H. D. Traill. Centenary Edition. 30 vols. London: Chapman and Hall, 1896–1901.

OTHERS

Abrams, M. H. *The Mirror and the Lamp: Romantic Theory and the Critical Tradition.* New York: Oxford Univ. Press, 1953.

Allen, Michael. *Poe and the British Magazine Tradition.* New York: Oxford Univ. Press, 1969.

Altick, Richard D. *The English Common Reader: A Social History of the Mass Reading Public, 1800–1900.* Chicago: Univ. of Chicago Press, 1957.

Bentley, Eric R. *A Century of Hero-Worship: A Study of the Idea of Heroism in Carlyle and Nietzsche, with Notes on Wagner, Spengler, Stefan George, and D. H. Lawrence.* 2nd ed. Boston: Beacon Press, 1957.

Booth, Wayne. *The Rhetoric of Fiction.* Chicago: Univ. of Chicago Press, 1961.

Burke, Kenneth. *Counter-Statement.* 2nd. ed. Berkeley: Univ. of California Press, 1968.

————. *A Grammar of Motives and A Rhetoric of Motives.* 1950; rpt. Cleveland: World Publishing Co., 1962.

Burwick, Frederick L. "Stylistic Continuity and Change in the

Prose of Thomas Carlyle." *Statistics and Style.* Math. Ling. and Auto. Lang. Processing 6. Ed. Lubomír Dolezel and Richard W. Bailey. New York: Amer. Elsevier, 1969. Pp. 178–96.

Calder, Grace J. *The Writing of Past and Present: A Study of Carlyle's Manuscripts.* Yale Studies in English, 112. New Haven: Yale Univ. Press, 1949.

Cassirer, Ernst. "The Preparation: Carlyle." *The Myth of the State.* New Haven: Yale Univ. Press, 1946. Pp. 189–223.

Cazamian, Louis. *Carlyle.* Tr. E. K. Brown. New York: Macmillan, 1932.

Cooper, Berenice. "A Comparison of *Quintus Fixlein* and *Sartor Resartus.*" *Trans. Wisconsin Acad. of Sciences, Arts, and Letters,* 47 (1958), 253–72.

Crane, Ronald S. "The Concept of Plot and the Plot of *Tom Jones.*" *Critics and Criticism.* Ed. R. S. Crane. Abridged ed. Chicago: Univ. of Chicago Press, 1957. Pp. 62–93.

Daiches, David. *Carlyle and the Victorian Dilemma.* Thomas Green Lectures, No. 4. Edinburgh: Carlyle Society, 1963.

Deen, Leonard W. "Irrational Form in *Sartor Resartus.*" *TSLL,* 5 (1963), 438–51.

Deneau, Daniel P. "The Relationship of Style and Device in *Sartor Resartus.*" *VN,* No. 17 (1960), pp. 17–20.

Dyer, Isaac Watson. *A Bibliography of Thomas Carlyle's Writings and Ana.* Portland, Me.: Southworth Press, 1928.

Eliot, George. "Thomas Carlyle." *Essays of George Eliot.* Ed. Thomas Pinney. London: Routledge and K. Paul, 1963. Pp. 212–15.

Fraser's Magazine. 1–10 (1830–1834). London: J. Fraser.

Froude, James Anthony. *Thomas Carlyle: A History of His Life in London, 1834–1881.* 2 vols. New York: Scribner's, 1884.

———. *Thomas Carlyle: A History of the First Forty Years of His Life, 1795–1835.* 2 vols. New York: Scribner's, 1882.

Frye, Northrop. *Anatomy of Criticism: Four Essays.* Princeton: Princeton Univ. Press, 1957.

Goldberg, Maxwell H. "Jeffrey: Mutilator of Carlyle's 'Burns'?" *PMLA,* 56 (1941), 466–71.

Goodheart, Eugene. "Goethe, Carlyle, and 'The Sorrows of Werther.' " *The Cult of the Ego: The Self in Modern Literature.* Chicago: Univ. of Chicago Press, 1968. Pp. 61–89.

Gordon, Mrs. [Mary]. *"Christopher North": A Memoir of John Wilson.* New York: W. J. Widdleton, 1870.

Grierson, Herbert J. C. "Thomas Carlyle." Annual Lecture on a Master Mind. *Proc. British Acad.,* 26 (1940), 301–25.

Harrold, Charles Frederick. *Carlyle and German Thought.* Yale Studies in English, 82. New Haven: Yale Univ. Press, 1934.

———. "The Mystical Element in Carlyle (1827–34)." *MP,* 39 (1932), 459–75.

———. "The Nature of Carlyle's Calvinism." *SP,* 33 (1936), 475–86.

Holland, Norman N. "Prose and Minds: A Psychoanalytic Approach to Non-Fiction." *The Art of Victorian Prose.* Ed. George Levine and William Madden. New York: Oxford Univ. Press, 1968. Pp. 314–37.

Holloway, John. *The Victorian Sage: Studies in Argument.* London: Macmillan, 1953.

Holmberg, Olle. "David Hume in Carlyle's *Sartor Resartus.*" *Arsberättelse,* 1933–1934 (Kungl. Humanistika Vetenskapssamsundet i Lund), pp. 91–109.

Houghton, Walter E. "Victorian Anti-Intellectualism." *Journal of the History of Ideas,* 13 (1952), 291–313.

———. *The Victorian Frame of Mind: 1830–1870.* New Haven: Yale Univ. Press, 1957.

Kennedy, George. *The Art of Persuasion in Greece.* Princeton: Princeton Univ. Press, 1963.

Kermode, Frank. *The Sense of an Ending: Studies in the Theory of Fiction.* New York: Oxford Univ. Press, 1967.

Langbaum, Robert. *The Poetry of Experience: The Dramatic Monologue in Modern Literary Tradition.* London: Chatto and Windus, 1957.

LaValley, Albert J. *Carlyle and the Idea of the Modern: Studies in Carlyle's Prophetic Literature and Its Relations to Blake, Nietzsche, Marx, and Others.* New Haven: Yale Univ. Press, 1968.

Lecky, William Edward Hartpole. "Carlyle's Message to His Age." *Historical and Political Essays.* New York: Longmans, Green, 1910. Pp. 95–105.

Levine, George. "Sartor Resartus and the Balance of Fiction." *The Boundaries of Fiction: Carlyle, Macaulay, Newman.* Princeton: Princeton Univ. Press, 1968. Pp. 19–78.

Levine, Richard A. "Carlyle as Poet: The Phoenix Image in 'Organic Filaments.' " *VN*, No. 25 (1964), pp. 18–20.

Lindberg, John. "The Artistic Unity of *Sartor Resartus.*" *VN*, No. 17 (1960), pp. 20–23.

McMaster, R. D. "Criticism of Civilization in the Structure of *Sartor Resartus.*" *UTQ*, 37 (1968), 268–80.

Marx, Leo. *The Machine in the Garden: Technology and the Pastoral Ideal in America.* New York: Oxford Univ. Press, 1964.

Metzger, Lore. "*Sartor Resartus*: A Victorian *Faust.*" *CL*, 13 (1961), 316–31.

Miles, Josephine. *Style and Proportion: The Language of Prose and Poetry.* Boston: Little, Brown, 1967.

Miyoshi, Masao. *The Divided Self: A Perspective on the Literature of the Victorians.* New York: New York University Press, 1969.

Moore, Carlisle. "The Persistence of Carlyle's 'Everlasting Yea.' " *MP*, 54 (1957), 187–96.

———. "*Sartor Resartus* and the Problem of Carlyle's 'Conversion.' " *PMLA*, 70 (1955), 662–81.

———. "Thomas Carlyle." *The English Romantic Poets and Essayists: A Review of Research and Criticism.* Ed. Carolyn Washburn Houtchens and Lawrence Huston Houtchens. Rev. ed. New York: Modern Lang. Assoc., 1966. Pp. 335–78.

———. "Thomas Carlyle and Fiction, 1822–1834." *Nineteenth Century Studies.* Ed. Herbert Davis, William C. DeVane, and R. C. Bald. Ithaca: Cornell Univ. Press, 1940. Pp. 131–77.

Muirhead, John H. "Carlyle's Transcendental Symbolism." *The Platonic Tradition in Anglo-Saxon Philosophy: Studies in the History of Idealism in England and America.* London: G. Allen and Unwin, 1931. Pp. 123–46.

Neff, Emory. *Carlyle.* New York: W. W. Norton, 1932.

Ohmann, Richard. "A Linguistic Appraisal of Victorian Style." *The Art of Victorian Prose.* Ed. George Levine and William Madden. New York: Oxford Univ. Press, 1968. Pp. 289–313.

Olson, Elder. "Rhetoric and the Appreciation of Pope." *MP*, 37 (1939), 13–35.

——. "William Empson, Contemporary Criticism, and Poetic Diction." *Critics and Criticism.* Ed. R. S. Crane. Abridged ed. Chicago: Univ. of Chicago Press, 1957. Pp. 24–61.

Pankhurst, Richard Kier Pethick. *The Saint-Simonians, Mill, and Carlyle: A Preface to Modern Thought.* London: Sidgwick and Jackson, 1957.

Peckham, Morse. *Beyond the Tragic Vision: The Quest for Identity in the Nineteenth Century.* New York: G. Braziller, 1962.

Peters, Robert Louis. "Some Illustrations of Carlyle's Symbolist Imagery." *VN*, No. 16 (1959), pp. 31–34.

Rader, Ralph W. "Literary Form in Factual Narrative: The Example of Boswell's *Johnson.*" *Essays in Eighteenth-Century Biography.* Ed. Philip B. Daghlian. Bloomington: Indiana Univ. Press, 1968. Pp. 3–42.

Roberts, Mark. "Carlyle and the Rhetoric of Unreason." *EIC*, 18 (1968), 397–419.

Roellinger, Francis X., Jr. "The Early Development of Carlyle's Style." *PMLA*, 72 (1957), 936–51.

Rosa, Matthew Whiting. *The Silver Fork School: Novels of Fashion Preceding "Vanity Fair."* New York: Columbia Univ. Press, 1936.

Ryan, Alvan S. "The Attitude Toward the Reader in Carlyle's *Sartor Resartus.*" *VN*, No. 23 (1963), pp. 15–16.

——. "Carlyle, Jeffrey, and the 'Helotage' Chapter of *Sartor Resartus.*" *VN*, No. 27 (1965), pp. 30–32.

Sacks, Sheldon. *Fiction and the Shape of Belief: A Study of*

Henry Fielding, with Glances at Swift, Johnson, and Rich-ardson. Berkeley: Univ. of California Press, 1964.

Sanders, Charles Richard. "The Byron Closed in *Sartor Re-sartus.*" *SIR*, 3 (1964), 77–108.

Sharrock, Roger. "Carlyle and the Sense of History." *E&S*, 19 (1966), 74–91.

Shine, Hill. *Carlyle and the Saint-Simonians: The Concept of Historical Periodicity.* Baltimore: Johns Hopkins Press, 1941.

————. *Carlyle's Early Reading to 1834, with an Introduc-tory Essay on his Intellectual Development.* Univ. of Ken-tucky Libraries, Occasional Contribution, No. 57. Lexing-ton: Univ. of Kentucky Libraries, 1953.

————. *Carlyle's Fusion of Poetry, History, and Religion by 1834.* Chapel Hill: Univ. of North Carolina Press, 1937.

Shumaker, Wayne. *English Autobiography: Its Emergence, Materials, and Form.* University of California English Stud-ies, 8. Berkeley: Univ. of California Press, 1954.

Smeed, J. W. "Carlyles Jean-Paul-Übersetzungen." *Deutsche Verteljahrsschrift für Literaturwissenschaft und Geistesge-schichte* (1961), pp. 262–79.

————. "Thomas Carlyle and Jean Paul Richter." *CL*, 16 (1964), 226–53.

Sterling, John. "Carlyle's Works." *London and Westminster Review*, 33 (1839), 1–68.

Sussman, Herbert. "Transcendentalism and the Machine: Thomas Carlyle." *Victorians and the Machine: The Lit-erary Response to Technology.* Cambridge, Mass.: Harvard Univ. Press, 1968. Pp. 13–40.

Tennyson, G[eorg] B. *Sartor Called Resartus: The Genesis, Structure, and Style of Thomas Carlyle's First Major Work.* Princeton: Princeton Univ. Press, 1965.

Thoreau, Henry D. "Thomas Carlyle and His Works." *Gra-ham's Magazine*, 30 (March 1847), 145–52 and (April 1847), 238–45.

Thrall, Miriam Mulford Hunt. *Rebellious Fraser's: Nol Yorke's Magazine in the Days of Maginn, Thackeray, and Carlyle.* New York: Columbia Univ. Press, 1934.

Tuveson, Ernest Lee. *The Imagination as a Means of Grace.* Berkeley: Univ. of California Press, 1960.

Watt, Ian. *The Rise of the Novel: Studies in Defoe, Richardson, and Fielding.* Berkeley: Univ. of California Press, 1957.

Weaver, Richard M. *The Ethics of Rhetoric.* Chicago: Henry Regnery Co., 1953.

Wellek, René. "Carlyle and the Philosophy of History." *PQ,* 23 (1944), 55–76.

————. "Thomas Carlyle." *The Age of Transition.* Vol. III of *A History of Modern Criticism, 1750–1950.* New Haven: Yale Univ. Press, 1965. Pp. 92–110.

Willey, Basil. *Nineteenth Century Studies: Coleridge to Matthew Arnold.* New York: Columbia Univ. Press, 1949.

Williams, Raymond. *Culture and Society, 1780–1950.* New York: Columbia Univ. Press, 1958.

Wilson, David Alec. *Carlyle to "The French Revolution."* Vol. II of *Life of Thomas Carlyle.* 6 vols. London: Kegan Paul, 1923–34.

Witte, William. "Carlyle's Conversion." *The Era of Goethe: Essays Presented to James Boyd.* Oxford: Blackwell, 1959. Pp. 174–93.

Young, Norwood. *Carlyle: His Rise and Fall.* London: Duckworth, 1927.

Index

sim; relation of his thought to form of *Sartor*, 12, 13–14, 89, 90–91, 106, 114n, 119–22; writing of "Thoughts on Clothes," 16–24 *passim*; his purpose in writing *Sartor*, 16, 25–45 *passim*; difficulty publishing *Sartor*, 16, 30–32; on form of "Thoughts," 20; invention of Teufelsdröckh, 20, 23, 24, 76–79; invention of Editor, 23–24, 76; sends "Thoughts" to Fraser, 24; expands "Thoughts on Clothes" into *Sartor*, 24–30 *passim*; distinguishes *Sartor* from *Wilhelm Meister*, 29; preparation of *Sartor* for *Fraser's*, 34, 36; emends *Sartor* after 1831, 36–37, 40, 43–44; his later attitude toward *Sartor*, 39–40, 41

—views: on novels, 2n; on rhetoric, 12n, 19n; on German literature, 17–18; on imitation, 19n; on *Fraser's*, 21, 25, 33–34, 39, 41; on Reform agitation, 28, 31, 34; on periodicals, 32; on his style, 39; on Byron and Goethe, 87; on the interest of a man's life, 87–88; on romantic love, 99–100; on woman, 100n; on inspiration, 107n; on oratory and rhetoric, 128n; on fictional devices, 46, 67n

Cassirer, Ernst, 149n, 183n; on autobiographical element in *Sartor*, 82; on unromantic in Carlyle, 121n

Cazamian, Louis, 6n

"Characteristics": quoted, 20, 128n

Clothes Philosophy: premises of, 8–9; mentioned *passim*

Crane, Ronald S., 8n
"Corn-Law Rhymes," 23
"Count Cagliostro," 23
Cox, R. G., 21n

Daiches, David, 114n, 183n
Dandyism: target in *Sartor*, 133, 164–65, 166–67
Deen, Leonard W., 4n, 116n; on disorder in *Sartor*, 119
Deneau, Daniel P., 2n, 68n
"Diamond Necklace," 67n
Dickens, Charles, 38; *Great Expectations*, 10, 49; *David Copperfield*, 91n
Die Kleider: functions of, 123–24, 125; mentioned *passim*
Diogenes, 18
Donaldson, John W., 137n
Dryden, John: fiction in *Essay of Dramatic Poesy*, 178
Duffy, Sir Charles Gavan, 43n
Dyer, Isaac Watson, 31n, 32, 40n, 43, 44, 123n

"Early German Literature," 27n
Edgeworth, Maria, 50
Edinburgh Review, 23, 71n, 76
Editor: invention of, 23–24, 76; Carlyle on, 34; as rhetorical device, 48–76; not distinct from Teufelsdröckh, 50, 56–58; coordinated with Teufelsdröckh, 58–70; effect on form, 74–75; functions of, 124–26, 131–32, 165–66; mentioned *passim*
Eliot, George: *Middlemarch*, 49; on *Sartor*, 185
Emerson, Ralph Waldo, 46; on *Sartor*, 6, 38–39; publishes *Sartor*, 31; on *Fraser's*, 38; questions Carlyle's rhetoric, 42; "Introduction" to *Sartor*, 44